Maggie Jackson's Kid

By the same author

The Stranger
The Forest Rangers

As ABC and/or BBC serials:

The Moon Flower, the First Planet, The Venus Adventure,
UFO 1400, The Ghost Car, Blue Water Blues,
The Three Lunateers, Mariners on the Moon, High Holiday,
The Windmill Mystery, Wallingford Castle,
The Gentry is Born, Wandjina, Beyond the Stars,
Operation Spaceman, The Star People

Maggie Jackson's Kid

G K Saunders

Aboriginal Studies Press
1998

FIRST PUBLISHED IN 1998 BY

Aboriginal Studies Press for the Australian Institute of Aboriginal and Torres Strait Islander Studies, GPO Box 553, Canberra ACT 2601

The views expressed in this publication are those of the authors and not necessarily those of the Australian Institute of Aboriginal and Torres Strait Islander Studies.

COVER ILLUSTRATION © *PEARL BECKETT 1998*

NATIONAL LIBRARY OF AUSTRALIA CATALOGUING-IN-PUBLICATION DATA:

Saunders, G K (George Kenneth)
Maggie Jackson's kid.

ISBN 0 8557 318 8.

I. Title.

A823.3

COVER BY Pearl Beckett

PRODUCED BY Aboriginal Studies Press

PRINTED IN AUSTRALIA BY Ligare Pty Ltd, Riverwood NSW

3000/6/98

To

Rebecca
Emily
Julia
and
Sarah

with love

Contents

Glossary

English underworld slang — circa 1820

a Botany Bay swell	an ex-convict after serving sentence
canary	a yellow-jacketed convict
a cleanskin or clean potato	a free citizen
crow	lookout (v. or n.)
crusher	policeman
to dab it up with	to live with (de facto)
dip, dipper	pickpocket
dollymop	a female prostitute
duds	clothing
a fakement	a faked act to distract from the real job
a flash pull	a big job
flummut	trouble, problems
fly	quick, sharp
glocky	stupid, mental
to get lushed	drunk
to go to ground	to hide
a hoof	a horse
knock it over	to do the job
a lackin	a respectable girl
the lay	the plan of a job
lurk	a trick or scheme
patter	smart talk, conversation
to peep	to keep watch
the pogue	the stolen goods
the pull	the job or crime
to put in lavender	to get rid of (kill)
to put up	to organise (a crime)

screwsman	key and safe specialist
to sing	to give the game away, to talk
a skirt	a female
square-rigged	respectable, proper
stall	a crook's accomplice who starts a fight to divert attention if required
a swell	a gentleman
a tightener	a good meal
a topping	an execution, a hanging
to voker or granny	to understand

All men are alike as a row of pins for the Colonel's lady and
Judy O'Grady are sisters under their skins.
Rudyard Kipling (1896)

....Those wonderful, humane people — primitive, yes,
but with a code of behaviour that puts to shame this
thing we call civilisation.
Peter Finch (1948)

Chapter 1

The Rescue

'Thomas! Come down this instant!' The girl's tone was sharp and assertive. 'You promised Papa you wouldn't climb up the rigging.'

Her young brother looked down at her defiantly. Prudence, he thought irritably, even at fifteen, sounded more like their mother every day.

'I shall tell!' she called, turning as though to carry out her threat at once.

'Oh, don't take on so!' the boy replied impatiently. 'The rigging is quite safe and I'm only up a little way. You can see the land better from up here.'

The bosun's voice, harsh and peremptory, rang out from the ship's bow. 'Hey, you! Come down off o' there, d'ye hear me?'

Startled, Thomas turned towards the voice. One foot slipped from the wet rope step of the ladder, the other followed and for a brief moment he hung by his hands. The ship rose on the swell and rolled heavily, swinging him out over the grey-green water. His numbed mind took in the tumbling sky and clouds as he pitched head over heels and, as in a nightmare, heard the shrill, distant scream of his sister. Then the cold water struck, closed over him and he felt himself sinking endlessly. For an age the cloying water held him then suddenly he broke the surface, his lungs near bursting. The empty ocean heaved before him. A great slow roller lifted him then he was engulfed once more. The following trough uncovered his head just long enough for him to take a deep, convulsive gulp of air before the green horror rolled over him again. The terrifying thought came to him that he was going to drown. Desperately he fought back and was briefly rewarded by a glimpse of blue sky and white clouds above imprisoning walls of water.

Suddenly his right arm was gripped as in a vice. He felt himself being lifted until his head was once more above the surface and he could suck in the sweet, warm air. As he and his rescuer rose together on a wave, he saw the ship, its grey, salt-stained sails hanging limply and flapping in the breeze. And the jolly-boat was already bobbing in the water alongside.

The surgeon-superintendent of the ship, Dr Middleton, was in the cabin of the children's parents, Mr and Mrs Weatherby. Eighteen weeks ago the *Lady Annabel* had sailed out of the Thames estuary and into a violent storm in the English Channel with some three hundred convicts down below and on the upper deck a dozen families of free settlers, including the Weatherbys. By Mrs Weatherby's account the voyage to New South Wales had been one long storm from then on. Storms there had been when the sea rose mountain high, sending great waves booming across the decks and swirling down the companionways, even flooding the passengers' cabins. The convicts, chained together in the black, airless holds, had often been knee-deep in water and wet through, to the great concern of Dr Middleton.

The storm of the last two days had now subsided and, though the ship still rolled heavily, the clouds had broken and a warm sun was shining. Best of all, the coast of New South Wales had appeared on the horizon. 'Come, ma'm,' the doctor was saying as he tried to cajole Mrs Weatherby into leaving the bunk in which she had spent most of the voyage. 'The coast is in sight and you will soon be safe on land again.'

'Alas,' Mrs Weatherby replied wearily, 'I am not accustomed to such conditions as exist on this ship, sir. I was brought up to better things. I am used to the services of a lady's maid.'

'And a lady's maid you shall have, ma'm,' the doctor declared cheerfully. 'I know the very person for you. I've had it in mind to recommend her to your notice for some time. Now we are soon to disembark I think you should make her acquaintance before some other settler's wife bespeaks her services.'

Mrs Weatherby raised herself modestly on one elbow, her languor suddenly dispelled. 'A lady's maid? On board this ship?'

'Perhaps not a lady's maid,' Middleton replied with a shrug, 'but a good, dependable young woman by the name of Mandy McInnes who could be schooled to suit you in no time, I'm sure.'

'You cannot mean that Scottish convict gel?' Mrs Weatherby asked, lowering herself slowly to her pillow as though in pain. 'The one who serves the lime juice to the female convicts on the afterdeck and calls out, "Time for your physic! Come along, ladies!!".' She gave a disdainful snort. 'Ladies, indeed!'

The doctor smiled. 'The same. An honest, reliable girl.'

'Honest, you say? But she's a convicted felon!'

Middleton restrained his rising impatience with difficulty. 'Where you and I are going to spend the rest of our lives, ma'm — I, too, for this is my fourth and last voyage — I fear you will find few others to employ. There are some female convicts who have much good in them and, among these, Mistress McInnes shines, I assure you. I recommend you to secure her for yourself while you can.'

Mr Weatherby patted his wife's hand gently. 'We should do well to rely on Dr Middleton's advice, I think, m'dear.'

The doctor picked up his black leather bag and turned with his hand on the door latch. I'll send her to see you and you may judge her character for yourself. She shall be relieved of all duties and placed entirely at your disposal.'

As he spoke a wild patter of feet sounded outside and the cabin door was flung open. Prudence, hair awry and eyes wide with terror, hurled herself into the arms of her astonished father. 'Thomas ... Thomas!' she managed to gasp. 'He's fallen into the sea!'

Chapter 2

A Brace of Convicts

By the time Dr Middleton and Mr Weatherby reached the open deck, Thomas and his rescuer were being hauled into the jolly-boat in the wake of the now stationary ship. Some fifteen minutes later Thomas was helped to scramble on to the deck, a sorry, bedraggled sight. His father quickly shepherded him below without so much as a glance at the burly convict who had followed the boy over the bulwarks, his dark hair plastered to his head and water dripping from his curly black beard. A young giant of a man in his late twenties, he stood aside as though hoping to go unnoticed while the crew of the jolly-boat spilled over the rail after him.

Dr Middleton strode up to him. 'So it was you, Morgan. I might have guessed.'

The man lowered his eyes. His lips, almost hidden beneath a drooping wet moustache, curved into a shy half smile. 'Oh, I enjoyed the swim, sir. First one I've had for a long time, look you,' he replied in a lilting Welsh accent.

'You'd best get out of those wet clothes,' Middleton said, steering him towards a companion-way leading to his own cabin. Morgan hesitated at the door but the doctor pushed him inside. He plucked a towel from a peg and tossed it to the convict. 'Strip off and dry yourself, man,' he said. 'I want to talk to you.' The doctor watched with a professional eye the play of the great muscles of the man's back and arms as he plied the towel vigorously. 'You were a blacksmith, weren't you, Morgan?' he asked casually.

'Blacksmith, carpenter, stonemason ... I was 'prenticed to a blacksmith but I'm a useful man with adze or scutch. I can shape iron, wood or stone, sir.'

The doctor nodded approvingly. 'A useful man, indeed!' He hesitated briefly then added, 'May one ask why you are here, Morgan?' The man straightened himself, his brown eyes fixed steadily on his questioner, but said nothing. 'You don't have to tell me,' Middleton added.

Morgan secured the towel around his waist. 'I don't mind telling you, sir. Not that I'm proud of what I did, you understand, but honest work wasn't possible to come by in the valley.' He paused, his mind suddenly thousands of miles away in his native Wales. 'Needs must when the devil drives, they say ... It was flying the blue pigeon as was my downfall, sir.'

'Flying the blue pigeon? What the devil does that mean?'

'Stealing old lead from the roof of a church. That's what it's called, sir. From a church as no one has set foot in this hundred year ... and me and me old mam without so much as a crust of bread.' A bitter note crept into his voice. 'Seven pennies I sold the lead for, sir. Seven coppers I got for it and seven years in Botany Bay. And the shame of it was the death of me old mam.'

The doctor shook his head sympathetically. 'I'm sorry, Morgan. But good may come of it yet, man. If I'm not mistaken, you'll spend the rest of your days in this new country...'

'Begging your pardon, sir,' Morgan interrupted, frowning, 'but when a man has served his term he's free to come and go as he pleases.'

'You misunderstand me,' Middleton explained quickly. 'When your seven years is up, I wager you won't want to return home. You'll make a good life for yourself here in New South Wales. See what a good start you've made, saving the life of a settler's young son even before you've set foot in the colony. I'm going to recommend you for a ticket-of-leave. Do you know what that means?'

'I've heard tell of it, sir. It's a sort of freedom...'

'It means that you won't be treated like other prisoners. You'll be free to seek work and earn money. In time you may even be granted land to make yourself independent as you could never hope to be in the old country if you lived to be a hundred.'

Morgan smiled broadly. 'I'd take kindly to that, sir, and no mistake!'

'Well, you may be sure I shall do my best on your behalf as soon as we reach Sydney. Perhaps you'd consider coming with Mr Weatherby and me and working for us to begin with, eh? We'd pay you well, Morgan.'

'Sir, I'll do that and be happy indeed if you can make it possible for me.' There was a knock on the door and Mr Weatherby entered. The sight of Morgan's massive form wrapped only in a towel surprised him and he stood uncertainly in the

7

doorway. 'Come in! Come in!' Middleton greeted him. He turned to Morgan, 'This is Mr Weatherby, the father of the boy whose life you saved. No doubt he's come to thank you.'

Morgan edged towards the door. 'I'll be off, sir,' he muttered uncomfortably. 'My duds will soon dry out in the sun.' The door closed behind him.

'That was the man?' Weatherby asked. The doctor nodded. 'I shall be eternally in his debt! However can I reward him?'

'You'll have your chance tomorrow when we berth in Port Jackson.'

'What is his name?'

'Morgan Jones, a young blacksmith from the Rhondda valley in South Wales. He's been one of my trusted helpers on this voyage. And tomorrow you can reward him by adding your strongest recommendation to mine when I present his application to the Governor for a ticket-of-leave. By the way, he has agreed to work for us.'

Weatherby frowned. 'Is that wise? Of what crime was he convicted?'

'A very trifling offence, I do assure you.'

'Ah, well. I must leave such decisions to your discretion. As for that convict gel you mentioned to my wife...'

'I hadn't forgotten. I shall see to it at once.' The doctor rose, opened the door and held it against the rolling of the ship as he gestured his visitor to precede him.

'I should be greatly obliged,' Mr Weatherby said. 'There is a good deal of packing to be done, you understand, and my wife is accustomed to having servants for such work.'

'I understand perfectly,' Middleton replied, a hint of irony in his voice. 'I'm sure it must be very difficult for a lady of Mrs Weatherby's breeding and upbringing to adjust herself to colonial conditions.'

Chapter 3

Mandy

Mrs Weatherby was dressed when a gentle tapping sounded on her cabin door. Her husband opened it. In the shadows of the narrow corridor stood a tall young woman of nineteen or twenty in the unbecoming grey overall of the female convict.

'Mr Weatherby?' she enquired softly. 'The doctor told me to come here'.

'Ah, to be sure,' Mr Weatherby replied. 'Mistress McInnes, is it not?'

'Aye, sir.'

He stood back to allow the girl to enter and closed the door behind her. He turned to his wife. 'This is Miss McInnes, m'dear, the gel the doctor spoke of.'

The English lady looked her up and down with studied disdain. 'H'mm, I see.' A pause, then, 'Turn around, gel. Turn right around slowly so that I may inspect you.' The girl did as she was asked. 'H'mm, are you clean?'

'As clean as can be, ma'm, considering...'

'Considering what, may I ask?' Mrs Weatherby interrupted coldly.

'I think what the young lady means, m'dear,' her husband explained, 'is that conditions below deck are not...'

'Mr Weatherby,' his wife broke in, 'let us come to an understanding at once about this convict person. Young she may be but a lady she most certainly is not. She is a convicted felon, a criminal, under sentence of transportation.'

'Quite! Quite so, m'dear,' her husband hastened to agree meekly.

The lady's supercilious gaze swept over the girl once again as she stood, waiting patiently, her natural dignity as unaffected by the words as if they had no reference to herself. 'What is your name, gel?'

'Mandy, m'am. Mandy McInnes, if you please.'

'Here you will be known simply as McInnes. Do you understand?'

'Aye, m'am.'

'You are here on sufferance, McInnes, on the recommendation of Dr Middleton. However, if you are industrious and obedient and keep a civil tongue in your head, I may request the authorities to allow you to work for me. Is that clearly understood?'

'Aye, m'am.'

'Very well. Then you may begin by packing this trunk under my supervision. I'll trouble you to wash your hands before you touch anything.'

Mandy remained standing still in the middle of the cramped cabin, her expression calm and self-possessed.

'Come along, gel!' Mrs Weatherby ordered sharply.

Mandy took a deep breath. 'Before I undertake to work for ye, m'am, there must be understanding on both sides. With respect to ye, m'am,' she went on quietly but firmly, 'but I am no criminal.'

Mrs Weatherby's eyes opened wide with surprise and indignation. Her husband, too, looked nonplussed. 'Do you mean to say, McInnes,' he demanded sternly, 'that you believe yourself to have been unjustly convicted?'

Mandy regarded him coolly with steady blue eyes. 'Convicted justly or not is beside the question, sir. What I did, I did and ask no pardon for it. I made them pay that robbed me and mine first. My conscience is clear on that score.' She turned to Mrs Weatherby who was sitting bolt upright on the edge of her bunk flapping a fan beneath her chin. 'If I am to work for ye, m'am, which I am right willing to do, having Dr Middleton's word as to your well-meaning, there must be goodwill and understanding on both sides. I make no pretence of being a lady but criminal I am not.' Mrs Weatherby seemed to have fanned herself into a state of quite unnatural speechlessness and continued to fan and stare as though unable or unwilling to believe her own ears. 'And now, m'am,' the girl concluded, 'if ye're still wishing it, I'm ready to attend upon ye.'

Mrs Weatherby flushed. Instinct told her she was going to need this girl's strength of body and mind in the life that lay ahead of her. Worst of all, she knew there was nothing she could say at that moment which would provide her with a dignity to match that of the convict girl.

Chapter 4
The Kid

Mrs Weatherby looked around hopelessly at the dingy little bedroom. Its furnishings were sparse, crude and mostly homemade. Only the double bed which took up most of the floor space showed signs of a former glory but now its elaborate brass-work was battered and tarnished.

The walls of the room were paper thin, mere wooden frames hung with sacking, once taut and whitewashed but now wrinkled and flaking. The landlady, a fat Irishwoman by the name of Mrs Ryan, had warned them cheerfully to keep their voices low if they didn't want their every word to be overheard by the other tenants in her little boarding house.

Thomas turned from the grimy window overlooking the narrow street. He had never before seen a wagon drawn by a team of bullocks and the slow progress of the great horned beasts as their hooves churned the ankle-deep mud fascinated him.

'We shall make the best of things here in the meantime,' his father said with forced good humour. 'I've been told there are quite comfortable cottages to be rented a few miles away in a village called ... Parra ... Parra something...'

'Parramatta, Papa,' Prudence informed him irritably as she whisked a persistent fly away from her perspiring face.

Her mother flapped her hands helplessly. 'Such outlandish names!' she complained. 'And such a primitive, outlandish place! It was bad enough that there were no cabs to be had at the quay-side, but to have to walk through those disgusting streets behind one's baggage piled high upon a handcart and then to end up in lodgings such as this with that dreadful Irish Ryan person...' Her husband made frantic silencing gestures towards the flimsy walls.

'Thomas ... Prudence!' he said sharply, 'kindly run downstairs and carry up as much of the hand luggage as you can manage between you. I'll be down to help you directly, as soon as I've made your mother comfortable.'

Thomas moved quickly towards the door but Prudence stood looking at her father in astonishment. 'Must we carry up our own luggage?' she asked incredulously.

'Alas, alas!' murmured Mrs Weatherby 'To think we have come to this!'

Thomas was already clattering down the bare wooden staircase. The family's baggage and a modest bundle tied with rope belonging to Mandy McInnes was piled on the narrow verandah near the front door where it had been dumped by the hand-cart's taciturn owner. Thomas waited for his sister in the bare passage at the foot of the stairs. As she joined him, a door in the passage flew open and the bulky figure of Mrs Ryan emerged with astonishing speed, her voluminous skirts and

14

petticoats held high, revealing bare, calloused feet. She lumbered past them and disappeared through the front door. 'Got ye, me fine boy!' they heard her cry as a shrill yelp of pain came from behind the pile of luggage just visible outside. 'It's no use of ye struggling with me. I'll not let ye go!' Loud slapping sounds punctuated her angry outbursts. 'Caught ye in the act, did I not, eh? I'll learn ye to come thievin' on my premises!'

Thomas and Prudence stared in astonishment at the spectacle on the verandah. Mrs Ryan, her triple chins trembling with the effort, was holding at arm's length what at first appeared to be a struggling bundle of dirty rags. 'There now!' she cried triumphantly. 'Will ye look at this now! Caught him red-handed, so I did, trying to make off with some of your duds from me own front porch!' The bundle of rags revealed itself as a dirty waif of a boy about the same age as Thomas. The boy stopped struggling and his defiant glare changed to a stare of astonishment as his eyes flicked from Thomas to Prudence and back as though they were creatures from another planet. Thomas stared back at the trapped urchin. He had felt the same way on the ship as he had watched the wretched convicts at their daily exercise on the afterdeck, unkempt, shambling and dispirited. There was no lack of spirit in this boy, though. He stared back at them boldly, even scornfully. Thomas was glad of that. Suddenly his mind was made up. 'I really think you are mistaken, Mrs Ryan,' he said.

Mrs Ryan looked puzzled. 'Mistaken is it? About this one? Now did I not see him through the window with me own two eyes lifting them bags and about to make off with them?'

Thomas gave his sister a furtive glance. 'But he was not about to steal them, m'am, I assure you,' he lied glibly.

'Thomas!' his sister exclaimed, 'what *are* you saying?'

'You see, m'am,' Thomas went on, ignoring her, 'in the absence of a manservant this boy was engaged to help my sister and me to carry these bags up to our rooms.'

Prudence stared at her brother open-mouthed. Mrs Ryan looked disconcerted. The whites of her captive's eyes shone against the ingrained dirt of his face.

'Is that the truth now?' the woman asked uncertainly. She gave her prisoner another shake. 'Helping, was it, ye young spawn of Satan? Then it's lucky for you the young gentleman spoke up when he did. It'd have been the lash for you else, I tell ye! But it's not the likes of yerself I'm wanting around my establishment so be off with ye!' She released her grip on his ragged collar and gave him a last resounding slap across the head with the back of her hand. The boy spat in her face then turned and ran away down the rutted road.

Mrs Ryan wiped the spittle from her face with a fat forearm as she faced Thomas. 'A fine one ye picked to help and no mistake! I'd as soon trust the devil himself as that brat of a boy!'

'I assure you,' Prudence began, 'we had not... ' Her brother cut her short. 'We had not heard of the boy's bad character, m'am,' he covered up quickly. 'We don't even know who he is.'

Mrs Ryan snorted. 'Then it's high time ye did for there's few hereabouts as don't. Maggie Jackson's kid, that's who he is, the young varmint!'

'And who might Maggie Jackson be, m'am?' Thomas asked before his sister could break in on the conversation again.

Mrs Ryan stumped across the rough wooden boards of the verandah. 'Who *was* she is more like it,' she leered, exposing stained and broken teeth. 'His mam's been dead and gone these many years. Transported she was for thieving, so they say, and that's how her kid keeps himself. 'Tis in the blood of him and if the blood's bad there's naught can be done about it, God rot the little sod!'

'But what of his father?' Thomas persisted, now genuinely interested. 'Does he not care for him?'

The woman turned at the front door. 'His father, is it?' She laughed scornfully. 'It's the same with himself as many others in this country — he don't know who his father was.'

She disappeared into the house and Thomas glanced at his sister sheepishly. 'I know what you're thinking,' he said, 'but I couldn't help it. I felt so sorry for him. He looked so poor and ragged and dirty.' He shook his head as if trying to dispel the memory. 'I just felt so sorry for him,' he repeated lamely.

Mr Weatherby's voice was heard calling them. 'Coming, Father!' Thomas answered, as he seized the two nearest canvas bags.

'Just wait till Mama and Papa hear of this,' Prudence remarked smugly.

'No. Pru! Please don't tell them!' her brother pleaded. 'No harm came of it. It was only a little white lie. Let it be our secret. I'll make it up to you, I promise.'

Prudence picked up a carpetbag and followed him to the door, a prim smile on her face. 'Very well,' she agreed. 'We'll see, but you'd better behave yourself in future or else...'

Chapter 5

Trial by Water

The tiny cottage with walls of tamped earth and roof of gum tree bark which Mr Weatherby had rented in Parramatta restored some privacy to the family though it provided little more comfort and convenience than Mrs Ryan's establishment.

With McInnes at her beck and call, Mrs Weatherby had coped remarkably well while her husband and Dr Middleton, each granted two thousand acres in the valley of the Hunter River, had set off to explore their land. Morgan, now a ticket-of-leaver, had gone with them.

When the men returned after several weeks, preparations for the final journey began in earnest. The expedition was equipped with two large bullock wagons loaded with stores and tools, a two-wheeled ox cart, a horse-drawn buggy for Mrs Weatherby, Prudence and Mandy and saddle horses for the men and Thomas. Forty convicts, assigned labourers, a mob of sheep, three milking cows, a young bull and several extra horses completed the company.

The first part of the journey, northwards up the coast to Newcastle, the coal mining settlement at the mouth of the Hunter River, was best made by sea. Mrs Weatherby was horrified at the prospect of more shipboard travel although the voyage took only two days but when the thunderous clamour of the sea had been replaced by the comforting crunch of buggy wheels, Mrs Weatherby, inspired by Mandy's firm hands on the reins and the retinue of assigned servants shambling along behind, became once more the master's lady.

Thomas attached himself to Morgan whenever he could, asking endless questions about the wide, trackless countryside through which they were passing. On the earlier journey Morgan had observed with wonder the tall, stately emus whose lanky, awkward looking legs carried them off like the wind at the approach of intruders. He had watched the little family groups of kangaroo and wallaby, staring suspiciously, ears erect and nostrils twitching, before bounding away in panic through the scrub. He had gazed in amazement at the flocks of gaudy parrots, the white cockatoos with their yellow crests and the pink and grey galahs that swooped and screamed above them in such excitement. His delight in their noise and antics was no less than Thomas's.

'Look, Morgan!' Thomas cried as a flock of parakeets flashed overhead in a rainbow torrent. 'Such beautiful birds! Do you suppose I might catch one and keep it in a cage? I might even teach it to talk!'

The Welshman shook his head. 'Now why would you want to do such a thing when the creatures are flying free all about you?'

'But I should like one for my own — a pet.'

'Why not make pets of them all, boyo?' Morgan suggested. 'If you were to feed them regular they'd be eating from your hand in no time, I shouldn't wonder.'

Prudence's voice brought the conversation to an end. 'Thomas!' she called sharply. 'Mama wishes to speak to you.' The boy turned his horse and waited till the buggy drew level.

His mother regarded him severely. 'Thomas, how many times have I told you not to make so free with that person, Morgan Jones? Kindly remember that he is a servant and not your equal.' Thomas opened his mouth to argue but his mother's uplifted hand stopped him. 'Please,' she went on crossly, 'don't take the trouble to remind me again that he saved your life. That makes no difference to his position as a common artisan and a criminal to boot.'

The boy returned his mother's gaze rebelliously. 'Morgan is no longer a convict, mother,' he pointed out firmly. 'He has a ticket-of-leave from the Governor.'

'Yes, yes, yes! I know that but it makes him no fit company for a child of mine. Kindly remember that.'

Thomas knew from experience that it would be useless to continue the conversation. He spurred his horse to join his father and Mr Weatherby who, with Morgan, were deep in discussion on the bank of a small river across the track. 'We forded this stream hereabouts before,' Dr Middleton was saying. 'It was a mere trickle then but look at it now! It must be thirty yards wide.'

'How shall we get across if the water is too deep?' Mr Weatherby asked anxiously.

Morgan studied the swiftly running stream, its normally clear water already tinged a muddy grey. From the stony bank at the water's edge the crossing already looked dangerous.

'Perhaps we should camp here until it subsides,' Mr Weatherby suggested.

Morgan shook his head and looked up to the lowering blue-grey storm clouds gathering on the horizon over the distant hills. 'It's raining hard up in the hills by the looks of it,' he said quietly. 'The stream will be in full spate by tomorrow, I shouldn't wonder.' He pointed to a nearby she-oak. Driftwood was lodged in its branches six feet from the ground. 'If we don't get across today we could still be waiting here in a week or more.'

Dr Middleton pulled out his pocket watch. 'Morgan is right,' he declared briskly. 'We have no more than four hours of daylight left. We must get across before dark or perhaps be held up for days.' He turned to the assigned men stretched out in the shade of the trees lining the creek. 'Who will volunteer to wade across?' he called. 'It may be necessary to swim for it.'

The men exchanged uncertain glances but no one spoke. Morgan stooped to unlace his boots but the doctor grasped his arm. 'No. I need you to drive the small ox-cart across. If we get that over safely the rest shouldn't be difficult. There must be other men here who can swim.' One of the convicts had risen. 'What's it worth then?' he asked challengingly.

Middleton looked the man up and down before replying. 'Jake Brightwell is your name, is it not?'

The man nodded. 'That's right.' Then, sensing he had gone a little too far, added, 'mister'.

'Can you swim, man?'

'Aye, but in that flow I'd be chancing me life.'

'Nonsense!' the doctor replied. 'You'd have a rope around your waist and if you got into trouble you'd be hauled out fast enough.' He waited for the man's decision. 'Well?' He looked steadily at him. 'Since you can swim, I have the authority to order you into the water. However, I won't do that. Instead, I shall reward anyone who volunteers with an extra ration of tobacco.'

A buzz of interest arose from the men and several stepped forward eagerly. Jake looked around at them resentfully.

Middleton pursed his lips to cover a smile. 'It seems we have more than enough swimmers,' he remarked, 'but since Jake Brightwell was the first to respond, he shall have the honour.'

The man's sullen expression changed. 'Thank ye, mister! Thank ye!' he exclaimed gratefully, reaching for the buckle of his belt as though anxious to be started in case the doctor should change his mind. Quickly he unbuttoned his moleskin trousers and was about to step out of them when a scandalised cry came from Mrs Weatherby in the buggy.

'Dr Middleton, sir! I protest! There are ladies present!'

Jake swiftly hoisted his moleskins up again and looked to the doctor for guidance.

Mrs Weatherby solved the problem for him. 'Prudence! Close your eyes!' she commanded. 'You, too, McInnes! Turn around both of you and follow me.' She climbed down unaided from the high seat of the buggy and led her two companions to sanctuary behind a bullock wagon.

Dr Middleton shrugged and turned back to direct operations. Jake undressed and Morgan looped a rope around his naked waist.

'When you get to the other side,' Morgan instructed him, 'take it off and tie it to a tree, real firm and tight, look you.'

The convict nodded and picked his way painfully over the stones and into the water. Suddenly a voice from the watching men broke the silence. 'Watch out for them crocodiles, Jake boy!'

Jake turned and stared in alarm at the group on the bank. The men laughed.

'Pay no heed!' Middleton called. 'There are no crocodiles in these rivers.'

'That's true, Jake,' the gruff voice agreed, laughing. 'Bloody sharks ate 'em all!'

The guffaw that followed was cut short by Middleton. 'That's enough!' he ordered sharply. All eyes followed Jake, now up to his thighs as he plunged forward into the current. Either he had not heard or he considered the sharks worthwhile risking for an extra ration of tobacco. He stumbled on, now halfway across, the water swirling around his waist as Morgan paid out the rope. His naked body slowly emerged as he staggered forward into shallow water, hampered by the heavy, wet rope still dragging in the current. At last he stumbled up the far bank, untied the rope from his waist and wound it around the trunk of a young tree. Then he sank exhausted into the grass. Morgan fastened his end of the rope to a large rock and regarded the bobbing lifeline with satisfaction.

'Do you think you could drive the two-wheeler across now, Morgan?' the doctor asked. 'It doesn't appear to be too deep.'

'I'm ready when you say the word.'

'Just a moment,' Weatherby said, grasping the doctor's arm as he turned to give the waiting men their orders. 'What about the ladies? You surely cannot expect Mrs Weatherby and Prudence to wade through waist deep water, especially in full view of all these men?'

'Then you and I must carry them.'

Weatherby looked shocked. 'That is quite out of the question! It would be undignified.'

'Are you suggesting we should leave them here?' the doctor asked impatiently.

'Of course not! But to carry them would be impossible in that current. The footing is too uncertain and neither Prudence nor my wife can swim.'

'Then they must take their chances in the buggy when the time comes,' Middleton replied with a shrug. 'At best they will get their feet wet; at worst, a ducking.'

The massive iron tyres of the small two-wheeled cart struck sparks from the stony creek bank as they rolled, clattering and scraping, towards the water. At the stream's edge the two bullocks stopped and lowered their heads to drink. Morgan made no attempt to urge them on. When they were satisfied they stood awhile, jaws dripping, and contemplated the swift current ahead as though judging the chances of a safe crossing. Suddenly Morgan's long whip snaked out, the lash cracking like a gunshot above their heads. 'Hup! Hup! Hup!' he shouted. The two powerful beasts lurched forward together, splashing through the shallows and plunging fearlessly into the strong undertow.

Animals and men stood watching in silence as the hubs of the big wheels disappeared under the swirling water and the bullocks stumbled forward holding their heads high. Even at the risk of catching sight of Jake's naked form on the far bank, Mrs Weatherby could not prevent herself from watching furtively.

The cart was now in the middle of the creek and taking the full force of the flood. The current pressed relentlessly against its half submerged side and swirled around it in a frothy whirlpool, scouring away at the loose stones of the creek bed under its wheels. The onlookers froze as the cart gave a sudden lurch and leaned over at a perilous angle. They saw Morgan leap from the driver's seat into the waist deep torrent, his stockwhip flailing the air furiously as he roared at the bullocks to keep them moving. Middleton hurled his hat on to the river bank and raced into the stream, shouting to the men to follow him. Certain of reward, a dozen or so plunged in after him, bounding and half swimming against the current until they reached the dangerously tilted cart, its tarpaulin-covered load now partly under water. Slowly but surely the drenched little band struggled towards the far bank, water cascading from the tailboard of the cart as it rose clear of the shallows and crunched over the dry shingle. Still breathless from their exertions, the men slumped to the ground and began to wring out their sodden clothes.

Middleton glanced down at his own clinging garments. 'Time for that later, men,' he called. 'There are still two wagons and a buggy to get across apart from the livestock. I'll see you're all dry again before we camp for the night.'

Morgan was standing beside the dripping cart, head on one side as though listening. The doctor squelched over to him and was about to speak but Morgan raised a hand to stop him. Both men stood listening. A faint, wailing cry was coming from under the tarpaulin, followed by a bout of coughing and retching.

The doctor pulled a sheath knife from his belt and slashed at the taut, shrunken ropes holding the canvas cover while Morgan hammered out the tailboard pins with a stone. As the tarpaulin was stripped away, Morgan wrenched the tailboard open. For a moment the two men stared in helpless astonishment at a bedraggled figure crouched in a nest of soaking blankets and blinking out at them through the long, matted hair that stuck to his grime-streaked face.

'My God!' Middleton exclaimed as they pulled the stowaway from his hiding place. 'This lad could have drowned! Who is he, in heaven's name?'

Morgan carried the boy to the grassy bank beyond the shingle and set him down carefully. He lay curled up awkwardly, convulsed at short intervals with bouts of vomiting. The doctor knelt down beside him, the centre of a curious circle of half-clothed men, dripping and steaming in the late afternoon sunshine. He looked around sternly at the ring of faces as he stripped the wet rags from the shivering lad. 'Who is this boy?' he demanded. 'How did he get into the cart? If any of you know anything about him, I warn you, you'd better speak up.'

Jake looked hard at the stowaway and his eyes narrowed. 'Don't know how the hell he got into the cart,' he said, 'but I know who he is, sure enough. That's Maggie Jackson's brat, that is.'

There was a muttered chorus of agreement from the men. Middleton placed a hand under the boy's chin and turned the grubby face up to him 'What's your name, boy?' The boy coughed but said nothing.

'I told ye, mister,' Jake said. 'They calls him Maggie Jackson's kid, 'cos he ain't got no proper handle. Leastwise, if he has no one's never got it out of him.' He appealed to the men. 'Ain't that so now?' The doctor frowned, puzzled. 'Don't you waste no pity on him, mister. He can fend for hisself, that one. A wild little bastard, he is. Goes and lives with the blacks whenever he wants. Eats snakes and grubs.' Jake spat noisily to show his disgust.

'How old do you suppose he is?'

'Thirteen, coming up fourteen,' the convict answered promptly.

Middleton looked surprised. 'You don't know his name but you sound very sure of his age.'

'I come out on the same ship as his mam. He was born on the ship. That's how I know.'

'Where is his mother now?'

'Dead, his mam is. She drownded herself in the Parramatta River, seven, eight years back. Tried to drownded him with her but the ferryman fished him out.'

'Then who has looked after him since?'

'I told ye,' Jake said impatiently. 'He fossicks for hisself. Never stays anywheres long. Thieves a few vittles then he's off again. Ye'll rue the day ye try to help that one, mister, I tell ye straight!'

The doctor looked down into the boy's cautiously watchful eyes and smiled. 'Ah, well,' he said. 'He seems to have recovered from his ordeal and he'll take no harm now in this warm sunshine. I'll decide what's to be done about him later. In the meantime there's a great deal of work ahead of us before nightfall so let's get on with it.'

Chapter 6

A Thief in the Night

Darkness was falling by the time men, beasts and vehicles were all safely on the other side of the rapidly rising creek. The two heavily loaded wagons had trundled irresistibly through the flood behind their long bullock teams. Only the buggy had been troublesome but eventually the pair of frightened horses, aided by twenty men on the end of a rope and Morgan's stockwhip cracking above their heads, had made a surprisingly speedy crossing. Now, with stars pricking the darkened sky, the Weatherby family sat silently beside the dying embers of the camp fire on which Mandy McInnes had cooked their evening meal.

Thomas yawned noisily, setting his sister off. Their mother noticed with tired approval that Prudence, unlike her brother, covered her mouth daintily with her hand. She was able to suppress an unladylike yawn herself only with a great effort.

'It's high time you were all in bed and asleep,' Mr Weatherby observed. He nodded towards the tent his wife shared with his daughter. Prudence made a half-hearted attempt to rise.

Thomas glanced over his shoulder. 'What about that boy?' he asked. Where will he sleep?'

His father looked about him into the deep shadows of the surrounding trees. 'Who?' he enquired in a puzzled tone. Thomas pointed to where the fitful light of the fire played on a small figure crouched in the tangled shadows of the scrubby bushes at the base of an ancient ironbark tree. 'The young stowaway, you mean?'

'Yes,' Thomas replied. 'He's been sitting there watching us all the time. Shouldn't we offer him some food or invite him to come a little closer and warm himself by the fire?'

His mother recoiled in horror at the suggestion. 'Certainly not! Let him share food and fire with the convicts. They are his class of persons.'

'He didn't eat with the convicts this evening,' Prudence reported with a meaningful look at her brother. 'I saw McInnes give him a great plateful of our stew. She was talking to him as well and they were both laughing.'

'Did she, indeed!' Mrs Weatherby responded sharply. 'Then I shall certainly have something to say to that gel in the morning!'

Thomas opened his mouth to defend Mandy but his resolution wilted as he caught his sister's smug smile and was reminded all too clearly of the incident on Mrs Ryan's verandah.

The little group around the fire looked up as Dr Middleton walked into the circle of light. 'I trust you have suffered no ill effects from your immersion in the river, sir?' Mrs Weatherby greeted him.

'No, m'am, I thank you,' the doctor replied cheerfully. 'A ducking was a small enough price to pay for a safe crossing without loss of man or beast.' He glanced at the small, shadowy figure at the base of the tree. 'It would seem that our party has even acquired a new member in consequence.'

'If you are referring to that disreputable little urchin who has been spying on us for the last hour, I think that is scarcely a matter for congratulation, sir.'

'He's gone!' Thomas exclaimed suddenly.

They all turned to look but the boy had slipped away as noiselessly as he had appeared.

Mrs Weatherby eyed the doctor critically. 'He should be placed under restraint with the convicts after dark,' she stated firmly.

'The lad is a free agent, m'am, not a prisoner,' Middleton replied. 'He may come and go as he pleases so long as he behaves himself. However, since he's chosen to join us I shall make myself responsible for his welfare and keep an eye on him. When all's said and done, he's just a boy of Thomas's age in need of the same care and attention.'

Mrs Weatherby bridled. 'Really, sir! I cannot conceive of any possible comparison between the needs of my son and that child.'

'Nevertheless, I regard the lad's health and well-being as of no less concern than Thomas's and so long as he chooses to remain with us I shall make it my business to ensure that he is provided with food, clothing and shelter and treated with humanity if not with civility.'

There was an awkward silence. Mr Weatherby smiled nervously. 'Won't you sit down, James, and join us for a while? What have you discovered about this extraordinary child? I confess he intrigues me.' Mrs Weatherby sighed heavily to show her disapproval of the subject but the doctor disregarded her.

'Little enough seems to be known about him,' he said. 'It appears that his mother's name was Jackson — Maggie Jackson — so presumably her Christian name was Margaret. She was transported for theft and the child was born on the voyage nearly fourteen years ago. This much I have on the authority of Jake Brightwell, a convict who came out on the same vessel. According to Jake, the woman kept very much to herself, refusing to discuss the child's father or to have very much to do with the other convict women who consequently made her life such a misery at the Women's Factory in Parramatta that when the child was about five years old she tried to drown herself and the boy with her. For her own part, poor soul, she succeeded but the child was rescued and, incredible as it may seem, has survived from that day to this largely by his own devices.'

'And is nothing more known about this Jackson woman?' Mr Weatherby enquired.

'Jake claims to remember her well. He describes her as reserved in her manner and ladylike.'

Mrs Weatherby sniffed. 'Reserved, possibly, but ladylike? Stuff and nonsense!'

'According to Jake,' the doctor continued, ignoring the interruption, she was said to have been maid and companion to a titled lady and was convicted of stealing from her.'

Mrs Weatherby rose with a superior smile. 'I bid you good night, sir. Come along, Prudence.' Her husband took her arm to escort her to their tent.

Left alone with the doctor, Thomas knew he could speak freely. 'Where will Maggie Jackson's kid sleep tonight?' he asked in a worried tone. 'He has no tent and no blankets. How will he keep warm? And if Mama orders McInnes not to feed him, what will he eat?'

Middleton placed a hand on the boy's shoulder and smiled at him reassuringly. 'Don't distress yourself on his account, Thomas. I've instructed Morgan to provide him with blankets and Jake Brightwell to keep an eye on him. As for food, no matter what your mother says, Mandy will see he doesn't go short.'

'Why do you suppose he wanted to come with us?' Thomas asked uneasily.

'That's a question I wish I could answer. He doesn't seem to be friendly with anyone in particular, except perhaps a little with Mandy.' The doctor paused. 'I've noticed him watching you closely, Thomas. Have you ever seen him before?'

Thomas reddened but the firelight disguised his blushes. 'Well ... yes,' he admitted reluctantly. 'I believe I saw him once in Sydney. But he would hardly follow us on that account, surely?' he added uneasily.

'Who can read the mind of such a strange, independent waif?' Middleton replied as Mr Weatherby rejoined them.

'I find it hard to believe that the boy has no given name,' Weatherby remarked as he took his seat near the fire. 'No mother could fail to give her child a name and the boy must surely remember it since he was five years old when his mother died.'

'Well, whatever name his mother gave him, he has steadfastly refused to reveal it...'

The three sprang to their feet as a piercing cry from Mrs Weatherby's tent shattered the calm of the night. They ran to the tent together.

'Mr Weatherby, I have been robbed!' his wife declared in ringing tones for all to hear.

'Robbed, m'dear? Surely you must be mistaken?'

'I am not mistaken, sir! The casket in which I keep my smaller items of jewellery has been stolen. Prudence will confirm that it was in its usual place beneath my pillow less than an hour ago.'

'Have you any suspicions as to the culprit, m'dear?'

'It would not surprise me if that wretched urchin were responsible.'

'But, Mama, he was sitting watching us beside the fire,' Thomas protested.

'He left suddenly a short while before Prudence and I retired,' his mother reminded him. 'Now we know why!'

'Jake Brightwell!' the doctor called loudly. 'Come here at once, man!'

Almost as though he'd been waiting to be called, the convict materialised out of the shadows. 'What's up, mister?' he asked gruffly.

'Where is that boy? I told you to keep an eye on him.'

Jake shrugged. 'I done my best, mister, but there ain't a man born could stalk that young skipper. What's he been up to, then?'

'A jewellery box belonging to Mrs Weatherby has been taken.'

'What did I tell ye?' Jake raised his hands in a gesture of hopelessness. 'Didn't I say ye dursn't trust that kid? If the lady's trinkets is gone ye can bet yer life that thieving young imp's got 'em.'

Middleton frowned. 'What makes you so sure of that?'

'Stands to reason, don't it? Which one of us'd be such a bloody fool?' the convict asked in an offended tone, indicating the men now crowding around. 'Any of us done a thing like that, us'd be lashed for it. Not him, though; he's a cleanskin, a currency lad, not Guv'mint like us.'

A low growl of agreement greeted this reply. There was logic in it, Middleton had to admit as he ordered the men back to their places.

'Well, what do you propose to do, sir?' Mrs Weatherby demanded when the men had gone.

'There is nothing to be done tonight, m'am,' the doctor replied, suppressing the irritation her air of triumph aroused in him. 'In the morning we shall find the boy and hear what he has to say. Justice shall be done, I promise you. Meanwhile, the lad remains innocent until proven guilty.'

Chapter 7

Information Received

Next morning the creek was running a banker and, as the sullen yellow torrent foamed around the lower branches of the she-oaks, each man silently congratulated himself on being safely across. Of Maggie Jackson's kid there was no sign but one thing was certain: he could not have gone back.

A mile or so into the new day's journey, Thomas left his horse in Morgan's charge and, made restless by the tedious, lumbering progress of the main party as well as a need for exercise, ran on ahead with Prudence. Mrs Weatherby, who rode in the buggy at the head of the column to avoid the billowing dust cloud that hovered over it, insisted that they stay within her sight. As they trotted together side by side, Thomas looked up delightedly at a pair of rowdy kookaburras in a tree above them.

'You call that dreadful noise laughter?' Prudence scoffed as the sound died away. 'Mama says that those birds must have been created by God to rebuke the evil-doers who are sent to this dreadful country.'

'Then why did father bring us here?' Thomas asked with sudden impatience. 'We are not evil-doers, are we?'

'Papa wishes to become rich, of course, silly!'

'But Papa was rich enough in England, wasn't he?'

Prudence gave him a pitying look. 'Really, you are such a duffer, Thomas! Papa was the younger son of a baronet so when grandfather died he inherited almost nothing. The estate and title both went to Uncle George and all poor Papa inherited was four thousand pounds.'

Thomas whistled. 'Four thousand pounds!' he exclaimed 'I should have thought that would have made him very rich.'

'Rich! On four thousand pounds?' the girl exclaimed scornfully. 'How long do you suppose that would support us in the style *we* are entitled to expect?'

'Then how has Papa become richer by travelling such a long way to all the hardships Mama complains of?'

'Because here in New South Wales, for every thousand pounds a man possesses he is given a thousand acres of land by the Governor as well as ten assigned servants, so Papa has paid for two thousand acres and one day we shall be able to live handsomely like the landed gentry do at home.'

'If that is so, why does Mama complain?'

'Because the country and the people are so disagreeable.'

'Well, I don't think the country is at all disagreeable,' Thomas retorted. 'Nor are the people.

Whatever Mama and you may say, I *like* Morgan — and McInnes, especially.'

'Then you must learn to keep such people in their place,' Prudence said. 'You cannot trust people of their sort. Take that frightful urchin in Sydney. You told a lie to protect him and how does he reward you? By stealing Mama's jewellery.'

Thomas had no answer to this for it appeared that Maggie Jackson's kid had confessed himself a thief by running away. Prudence glanced over her shoulder. 'Thomas!' she cried, 'we've come too far. The buggy is not in sight!'

They'll soon catch us up,' he replied, unconcerned.

'I think we should go back and meet them... Please, Thomas!'

'You can go back if you want to,' he said with a shrug. 'I'm going on as far as that big rock just ahead. I'll wait for you there.' He began to walk quickly away.

'If you leave me I shall tell,' his sister called. 'I shall tell Papa what you did in Sydney!' Thomas walked jauntily on as though he had not heard then suddenly stopped and stood quite still, staring at something on the flat surface of the big rock. He bent down to look more closely then picked up a small square blue object. Curiosity overcoming her fear, Prudence ran to join him. He turned, eyes wide with wonder as she came up to him, and held the object out to her. 'Look! Look, Pru! Look what I've found! Mama's trinket box!'

She stared at the small blue box in astonishment, then took it from him and struggled with the silver catch. The box was empty. Their eyes met, bewilderment in his, indignation in hers.

'That wicked, wicked creature!' she cried. 'He has stolen Mama's jewels and thrown away the box!'

'But it wasn't thrown away,' Thomas pointed out. 'It was sitting just here, plain for anyone to see, exactly as if it had been put there purposely.'

Mr Weatherby was riding alongside the buggy as the two children ran back to meet them.

'Look what we found!' Prudence cried breathlessly.

Mandy reined in the horses. She leaned down, took the box from Prudence and handed it to Mrs Weatherby who opened it eagerly.

'Empty!' she exclaimed. 'Where did you find it?'

'It was sitting on a big, flat rock for all to see quite plainly,' Thomas replied excitedly. 'It must have been put there on purpose for nobody could have missed it.'

Dr Middleton had cantered up to find out why they had stopped. Morgan was close behind him with the leading bullock wagon. He stood watching beside his beasts under a rolling cloud of dust.

'What do you make of it, James?' Mr Weatherby asked, handing the box over. 'Why should the thief leave the box where it was sure to be found?'

The doctor shook his head then, wheeling his horse, he shouted for Jake. The convict jumped down from the second wagon. 'What's up? Why we stopped here ...?' He broke off, his eyes narrowing as he saw the box in the doctor's hand. 'Where d'ye find that?' he demanded suspiciously. Middleton explained in a few words. 'You seem to know more about the boy than anyone,' he went on. 'Have you any idea why he should have left the empty box beside the track where it was certain to be noticed as we passed this way?'

'How the hell should I know, mister?' Jake replied quickly. 'The kid's glocky, I tell ye.' He tapped the side of his head with a grimy, calloused finger. 'Glocky. Soft in the head, see? Anyone in his right mind would have slung it away where it wouldn't never be found.'

Middleton nodded. 'Very well. Get back to your wagon. We must keep moving.'

Morgan placed a hand on the doctor's stirrup. 'If Jake never set eyes on that little box before,' he remarked, 'how did he know what it was without anyone telling him?'

Middleton shook his head. 'The same thought came to me, but what else could such a thing have been out here in the wilderness? I'm afraid there can be little doubt who the thief is, Morgan,' he added regretfully.

They pitched camp that evening on a low plateau well above the Hunter River, now swollen with the outpourings of dozens of small creeks set in flood by the rain on the nearby hills.

When Mandy was finally free to retire to her own tent, she fell at once into the deep sleep of the exhausted. It seemed to her that only a few minutes had passed before she was awakened by an urgent whisper. 'Hey, miss! Wake up!' She thought she must have been dreaming and closed her eyes again in relief. Then she felt a gentle touch on her shoulder and recoiled, instantly wide awake.

'Don't be feared, miss.' the whispered voice continued. 'It's only me — the kid. I ain't going to hurt ye.'

Mandy sat up, staring at a dim form in the darkness, her fright giving way to curiosity. 'Ye should be ashamed, ye young rapscallion!' she admonished him, matching his own soft whisper. 'Have ye brought back the trinkets ye stole, is that it?'

'No!'

'Then I'll have no truck with ye,' she declared firmly, throwing back the blankets.

'If ye calls 'em I'll be gone and I won't come back,' he warned. 'Then the old woman won't never see her sparklers again!'

'What d'ye mean by that, ye wicked wee devil?'

'I never vamped them sparklers, miss, cross me heart! But I seen who pulled the job and I seen where he planted the pogue. My oath, miss!'

The boy's earnestness was convincing. 'Then why d'ye come to me with it?' Mandy asked, her manner softening. 'Why don't ye go straight to Dr Middleton and tell him?'

'Agh! Ye're glocky like the rest of 'em,' the boy replied witheringly. 'Why d'ye think I went to ground like I done? If the cove as pulled the job knowed I'd blabbed on him, he'd bump me off, quick as look!'

'Bump you off?' Mandy repeated, mystified.

'Aye! Cut me bloody froat, he would!'

It took a moment for this dramatic information to sink in. 'Then tell me who it was and where the stuff is hid,' Mandy whispered, 'and I'll tell the doctor. But none of your lies now or you'll make me as bad as yourself.'

42

Chapter 8

Set a Thief

Dr Middleton, riding slowly along with the sheep, was surprised to find Mandy McInnes walking beside him. Glad of the opportunity to talk, he dismounted at once. 'Good morning, Mandy,' he greeted her warmly. 'I've not seen much of you lately. Mrs Weatherby seems to keep you pretty busy.'

Mandy smiled. 'Busy enough, sir.'

'Is there something you wish to talk to me about?' he asked quietly.

'Maggie Jackson's kid, sir.'

'Oh? What of him?'

'He came to me in the night, sir, with a message for you.'

'Did he, indeed? And you let him go away?'

'Aye, sir. I had no choice. If I'd tried to hold him he'd not have given me the message. It concerns Mrs Weatherby's trinkets, sir.'

Middleton listened in silence, his face clouding as she revealed the information she had been given in the night. It took only a few minutes and the doctor looked grim as she finished. 'If he's telling the truth,' he said, 'the real villain must never know who gave him away.' He paused, frowning. 'I must talk with Morgan. We'll think of a way to test his story.' He watched her run forward to catch up with the buggy then hoisted himself into the saddle and trotted over to Morgan's wagon.

That evening, after the Weatherbys had retired to their tents, Morgan rounded up the convicts for a medical inspection. He formed them up in two lines facing each other in a clearing where Dr Middleton was busy beside a small trunk containing his instruments and medicines. When the men were ready the doctor walked slowly between the rows. 'You will all remove your shirts so that I can examine you for insect bites,' he announced.

A flurry of activity followed as shirts and jackets were pulled off. The doctor, with Morgan carrying a lantern, walked slowly along one line and back along the other, inspecting each man as he passed. Some he told to dress again but others he ordered to remain as they were, ready for treatment. At last he found himself looking at Jake Brightwell's stubbly face. 'Why haven't you taken off your shirt?' Middleton asked sternly.

'Cos I ain't been bit,' the convict replied, a note of bravado in his manner.

'I'll be the judge of that, man. Off with it!'

Jake stared steadily back but made no move. Morgan put down his lantern and took a purposeful step towards the convict. Suddenly the man turned his back on them and dragged his shirt around his neck, making a great show of pulling it over his head. Finally he placed it, carefully folded, at his feet. Middleton walked slowly around him. Jake waited with undisguised impatience.

At last they came face to face again. 'You seem to have lost your tobacco pouch,' the doctor remarked casually. 'I thought you kept it slung around your neck as the other men do.'

Morgan stirred the folded shirt with his foot, revealing a thin leather thong coiled beneath it.

'There's careless you are,' he said, bending to pick up the thong. 'You pulled off your tobacco pouch with your shirt, look you...'

Jake kicked his hand aside swiftly. 'Leave it be!' he snapped. He stooped to pick up his shirt but Morgan got to it first. The Welshman straightened, shirt in one hand and the bulging tobacco pouch in the other. He tossed the shirt to Jake and handed the pouch to Middleton. Jake regarded the doctor tensely as he hefted the pouch in the palm of his hand.

Middleton looked the convict in the eyes. 'You smoke an uncommonly heavy tobacco.' As he spoke he loosened the leather cord and opened the pouch.

Jake took a step forward but Morgan's muscular arm barred the way. Alarm spread across the man's face. 'Hey!' he protested with forced indignation. 'You got no call to vamp a man's baccy!'

He looked around him desperately, hoping for some sign of support from the others but they were too intent on watching the doctor as he spread a white towel over the lid of the trunk and emptied the pouch on to it. A small heap of roughly sliced tobacco tumbled out, followed by a trickle of small shiny objects that glittered in the light from the lamp

Morgan held up. The men broke ranks to get a closer view.

Middleton picked up a pair of sapphire ear-rings and several other small items of jewellery, separated them from the clinging tobacco crumbs and held them out in the palm of his hand for all to see. Suddenly all eyes were on Jake.

'I never knowed they was there!' he cried, 'I never knowed they was there, so help me! They was planted on me by the thieving sod what took 'em! I swear to God, mister!'

The doctor glanced down at the glittering items in his hand. 'Do you really expect me to believe that you didn't know these things were hidden in your tobacco pouch?'

'If God was to strike me dead, mister, I never knowed they was there! They was planted on me, I tell ye!'

A hostile growl arose from the other convicts at the repeated suggestion that one of them was the thief. Jake suddenly realised his mistake. 'No! No!' he cried. 'I never meant it was one of youse! It was that bloody kid, that's who done it. He must have took 'em and planted 'em on me, see?'

'Don't make it worse, man,' Middleton said coldly. 'You know the boy had nothing to do with it. Take him away, Morgan.' He turned to the other men crowded around. 'Get back to your lines. Some of you are still in need of attention.'

He watched with pity as Morgan led Jake away. He thought that if that insensitive woman had not flaunted her paltry baubles before the men, Jake might never have been tempted.

46

An hour later the doctor stood at the entrance of the tent shared by Thomas and his father. 'Are you awake, Henry?' he called softly.

The flap of the tent parted and Weatherby stood in the opening, a blanket thrown over his long nightshirt. 'I heard you addressing the men earlier,' he said. 'Is all well?'

'A medical inspection,' Middleton explained. 'However, I took advantage of it to get these back for your wife.'

Weatherby stared, speechless, at the little pile of jewellery in a handkerchief which the doctor held out to him. 'Wherever did you find these?' he asked in amazement. 'These things were stolen and the culprit must be punished.'

'He shall be.'

'It was that boy, of course.'

'No, it was Jake Brightwell.'

Weatherby's jaw dropped. 'Good God! How did you find out?'

'Certain information came to me indirectly by someone who saw him take the box, conceal the contents and throw the box away.'

'Then whoever gave you that information must be rewarded. Who was it?'

'That I cannot tell you because if Jake ever found out who the informer was he might even try to kill him.'

Weatherby looked stunned as a sudden realisation of the dangerous, violent nature of his adopted land flooded over him. 'Do you really mean that?' he breathed. The doctor's grim face was sufficient answer.

'How will he be punished? The lash?'

'I'm afraid so. I was warned that the fellow was an incorrigible trouble-maker but in my arrogance I thought I should be able to appeal to some streak of decency which I believe exists in every man.' He sighed. 'But not, it seems, in Jake Brightwell, so he will have to take his punishment.'

'You need have no qualms of conscience about it, James. You have been commissioned as a civil magistrate and you must do your duty.'

'If it were up to me,' the doctor said, 'I should not be so concerned for the fellow. But as a magistrate I am not empowered to judge or sentence my own assigned servants. I must take them to another magistrate and the nearest to us here is Major Murdoch, whose property we shall reach tomorrow.'

'So Major Murdoch will relieve you of an unpleasant task,' Weatherby pointed out.

'That is so,' the doctor agreed without enthusiasm. 'Alas for poor Jake! The major has an appalling reputation. The severest punishment a civil magistrate can order is fifty lashes. They say Murdoch never settles for less.'

Chapter 9

The Major

Next day, late in the afternoon, as they came in sight of the Murdoch homestead, the doctor and Mr Weatherby rode ahead to announce their arrival. On nearing the group of small but well-tended wooden buildings, the first they had come to as they followed the river from the coast, they were greeted by a noisy trio of bloodhounds. As the great dogs leaped at their shying horses they were called off by a loud bellow from Major Murdoch himself on the verandah of the whitewashed homestead building.

The major, a short, tubby Napoleonic figure with a florid complexion heightened by fluffy, white sidewhiskers, trotted towards them, watched warily by several men hoeing in the neat vegetable garden. He made no attempt to lower his voice. 'Sorry about the damned dogs! I'd have had 'em chained up if I'd known you were arriving today. Can't be too careful, y'know, when you're surrounded by ruffians and cut-throats. You'll find that out for yourselves soon enough, by Gad!'

Mrs Weatherby arrived a little later and as the travel-stained buggy crunched to a stop on the river gravel of the driveway at the front door, she was deeply impressed by the six female house servants lined up on the verandah behind her host and his lady. Conscious of so many eyes upon her, she descended from the high seat of the dusty vehicle, assisted by the major himself in an elaborate display of gallantry. Mrs Weatherby responded with a grateful smile and a dignified inclination of the head. It was a long time since she had been treated in the style she regarded as her due.

Darkness was falling by the time camp had been set up and Dr Middleton was free to join the Weatherbys in the simple comfort of the Murdoch home.

The major insisted on apologising loudly for the shortcomings of its rustic simplicity. 'Oh, I have plans!' he boomed. 'I have plans, by Gad, yes! The first brickmaker to walk off a transport in Sydney will be out of his chains and up here before you can say Jack Robinson. Oh, yes! There's good clay in the valley and I intend to build a grand brick house as soon as I have the man to do it.'

After supper, when the three men were alone, the conversation turned to Jake's crime. 'You can count on me, m'dear fella. I'll see the wretch gets his just desserts,' the major assured them. A new thought suddenly struck him. 'By Gad, Middleton, as a commissioned magistrate living in the district, you'll be able to do the honours for my malefactors, what?'

'Alas, yes,' the doctor replied with distaste. 'It is not a duty I look forward to but the need for it was explained to me by the Governor in Sydney.'

'Oh, you'll soon get the hang of it,' Murdoch assured him cheerfully.

In the morning, a table with a Union Jack was set up in the forecourt facing the wooden triangle to which the wrong-doers were tied for flogging. The major had arranged that Jake should have a show trial, witnessed by all the convicts including as many of his own as could be spared from their labours. As he explained to his visitors, a lashing watched was a lashing shared and the more thoroughly the men were cowed by such sights the better.

The convicts shambled into the courtyard, a surly audience. Dr Middleton followed the major as he marched importantly to the table and took his seat. He placed a heavy leather bound book before him and opened it. An unnatural silence fell upon the scene. Even the irreverent kookaburras watched silently. Major Murdoch glanced up at the doctor standing beside him. 'Bring out your man,' he ordered brusquely.

'Jake Brightwell, step forward!' Middleton called.

Jake shuffled towards the table, the short chain between his leg-irons dragging in the dust. He stood before the red, white and blue table, a pathetic, cringing figure, dread in his stance as in his drawn, grey-stubbled face. The major looked him up and down contemptuously.

The 'trial' was quickly over. The major's manner as he delivered the inevitable verdict and pronounced his routine sentence was brisk and uncaring. 'I'm sorry to say the law permits me to sentence you to no more than fifty lashes.' He paused, savouring the effect on the prisoner. 'Fifty lashes, you hear, man, eh?' he went on, his voice rising angrily.

Jake's face was ashen. He managed to nod almost imperceptibly.

'And I can tell you this,' the major went on in high indignation, 'if it were not for weakness and sentimental twaddle in Sydney and Westminster, it would be a hundred and fifty! And I've got a good scourger for this kind of work!' He looked around threateningly at the brooding circle of men, his white side whiskers bristling, then back to Jake. 'Carry out the sentence!' he barked.

Two of the major's men stepped forward, grasped Jake by the arms and half dragged him towards the triangle, pulling him up impatiently as he stumbled over his leg irons. They ripped the coarse linen shirt from his back and, having fastened his wrists to the top of the triangle with leather straps, hauled them tight so he was brought up on to his toes and hung from the wooden frame, his head drooping helplessly on his chest.

To Thomas, standing on a tree stump at Morgan's side, Jake appeared to be dead. The boy looked anxiously up at his companion. Morgan shrugged. 'You'll see it sooner or later, boyo,' he said, resting a reassuring hand on his shoulder. 'You can close your eyes if you choose but you'll not be able to close your ears.'

'Do you really think I should watch?' Thomas asked nervously.

'That's up to you, boyo.'

Thomas turned unhappily to where Jake was spread-eagled across the wooden triangle. The scourger, a stocky little man, stripped to the waist, muscles rippling beneath the thick black hair of his chest and abdomen, walked slowly towards his victim. His right hand gripped the cat-o'-nine-tails — a short wooden handle from which sprouted long leather straps tapering to points at the end and blackened with long usage.

'Will it draw blood, Morgan?'

'Oh, yes! It will draw blood, indeed,' Morgan replied grimly. 'And the blood will run down his back into his boots. And them little ants, they'll come scurrying around to pick up the bits of bloody skin that flicks off the lash and they'll hurry off with them back to their holes.'

Thomas felt his stomach turning. He jumped down from the stump. 'I won't watch! I won't watch!' he whispered in great distress. He stood close beside Morgan, his back to the scene, and stared out across the peaceful grey-green valley under a flawless sky of silky blue. Morgan covered the boy's shoulders with a brawny arm.

The cat-o'-nine-tails landed with a vicious slashing sound. Jake's body tensed and heaved as the blow fell then hung again as if lifeless. He made no sound. Thomas pressed his fingers into his ears. At the fourth blow, Jake grunted. At the fifth and sixth he screamed as red weals, swollen with blood, rose like malignant growths across his back. On the seventh stroke the weals burst and the cat's leather lashes, now wet and sticky with blood, fell back on to the dusty gravel surface of the forecourt. Slowly and deliberately the scourger drew them over the gravel, flicking them over and over until they were coated with fine grit. He raised his arm for an eighth blow as Dr Middleton's voice rang out.

'That will be enough!'

The scourger slowly lowered his arm and looked for guidance to Major Murdoch who, mouth open with astonishment, was standing beside the flag-draped table. 'What the devil!' he exclaimed, striding towards the doctor. 'The fella's only had seven strokes, dammit! He has another forty three to come!'

'I order the flogging to be stopped,' Middleton stated firmly.

'On what authority do you so order, sir?' the major demanded, his face purpling. 'As the magistrate acting in this case, what I decide is law!'

'And I am a surgeon. You will find that my authority in that capacity overrides yours as a civil magistrate where the health of a prisoner is concerned. That also was explained to me by the Governor.'

Murdoch glanced at Jake's blood-streaked back. 'Health?' he blustered 'Dammit, sir, that fella's as healthy as an ox. It'll improve his health to have a little of his rebellious blood let!'

For answer the doctor took the cat-o'-nine-tails from the scourger and held the filthy leather thongs out for the major's inspection. 'Have you ever examined this instrument?' he asked in an ominously quiet voice.

'Why the devil should I? I leave that to the scourger. All I want to know is that it's doing its work. Well, you heard the fella howl, didn't you? That's all the proof I need!' The major was beside himself with rage. Never before had his authority been challenged publicly and it was especially galling in front of the silently gloating audience of his own work force. He gestured to the scourger to continue but the cat was no longer in the man's possession. The scourger looked confused.

Middleton gathered the leather strips together in one hand and regarded the bundle distastefully. 'I will not allow any man's back to be cut by thongs in this rank and foetid condition. Dirt forced into a wound is the prime cause of putrefaction and gangrene. A man could die of blood-poisoning after a lashing with a cat-o'-nine-tails like this.'

The major could see it would be useless to continue to argue. 'Very well, sir,' he conceded in a belated attempt to restore some of his lost dignity. 'In medical matters I grant you have the final authority. So be it. But, by heaven, I warn you, you'll have trouble on your hands if you get yourself a name for being soft. These aren't ordinary men you're dealing with, y'know. These are the scum of humanity!' He stalked off towards his house, snatching up his great book of crimes and punishments from the table in passing. He slammed the door behind him as a subdued babble of malicious glee rolled through the assembled convicts.

The doctor looked around for Morgan who pushed his way into the clearing near the triangle. 'Help me cut him down, Morgan.'

Jake raised his head, his bloodshot eyes filled with tears. 'God bless ye, mister!' he gasped in a hoarse whisper. 'I won't forget what ye done this day, I swear! Ye'll not be sorry, mister. I'll be yer true man from this on, God curse me if I ain't!'

Morgan's strong arms caught him as the rawhide straps slackened and he slumped to the ground.

Chapter 10

The Squatter

It had been intended that the whole party should rest up for a couple of days on the Murdoch property but, after the events of the morning, this arrangement had been quietly forgotten. In the middle of the afternoon, Middleton gave the order to stop and set up camp for the night.

'Why are we stopping?' Mr Weatherby wanted to know. 'If we continued for a little longer we could easily reach the place we selected for our home before dark.'

The doctor smiled understandingly. 'Quite so,' he agreed, 'but we should all arrive dog-tired and your good lady would be in no state to appreciate the advantages of the site you have chosen. No harm in a little strategy, Henry. Better we arrive in the forenoon tomorrow when we're all still fresh and rested.'

When camp had been established, Thomas set out on the one chore permitted by his mother — the gathering of firewood. He came upon Morgan, standing alone on a grassy knoll, gazing intently up the valley. 'How much further is it to our land, Morgan?' the boy asked.

The blacksmith looked down at him in surprise. 'Haven't they told you? This is your father's land we're standing on. And yours one day, boyo.'

'You mean this is where we shall build our house? Here?'

'There's impatient you are,' Morgan chided him with a smile. 'We've a way to go yet before we reach the place your da' chose for his house.' He pointed to a ring-barked tree standing stark and lifeless on the river bank below them. 'See that dead tree? That marks the end of Major Murdoch's land and the beginning of your da's own... Two thousand acres,' he mused, shaking his head in wonder. 'Do you know how much land that is, boyo?'

'Enough to make my father a rich man?' Thomas asked hopefully.

'There's many a fine gentleman living in high style back home would be content to own two thousand acres of such land as this, I tell you. Any man who owns the land he stands on is a rich man,' Morgan replied with feeling. 'Two acres or two thousand, it makes no difference.'

Morgan resumed his steady gaze up the valley. Thomas could see only rolling grass land and trees. 'What are you looking at, Morgan?' he asked.

'Don't you see 'em, boyo? Them little white dots on the hillside — you know what they are?'

Thomas noticed the white dots for the first time. 'They look like sheep,' he said. 'They must have strayed from Major Murdoch's flock.'

Morgan shook his head. 'No, they're not strays. If you look real close you'll see there's a shepherd with them. A squatter, I shouldn't wonder.'

'A squatter? What's that?'

'A squatter,' Morgan replied, choosing his words carefully, 'is a landless man like myself who sees all this good pasture lying idle and puts it to good use for himself without troubling the Governor in Sydney town about it.'

When the news of the squatter was brought back to the camp, Mr Weatherby was deeply concerned. 'Don't upset yourself about it, Henry.' Middleton advised. 'He'll have to move on when he discovers the land he is using is now legally yours.'

'I should hope so, indeed!' Mrs Weatherby put in indignantly. 'He must be sent about his business at once!'

'Quite so! Quite so!' Middleton hastened to agree. 'But away out here we are beyond the protection of the law in the meantime so we had best try to settle the matter amicably. It might even be wise to offer the fellow some small compensation.'

'What? Pay the scoundrel to leave our own property?' Mrs Weatherby protested. She looked at her husband for support.

'He will have to go,' Weatherby said firmly.

'And what if the fellow refuses to move?' Middleton asked.

'Then he will have to be driven off. By force, if necessary. I have the men,' Weatherby pointed out.

The shadow of a derisive smile crossed the doctor's face. 'Oh, yes, you have the men,' he agreed readily, 'but do you have their goodwill in a matter of this sort? The man who owns those sheep, Henry, was almost certainly a convict himself; one who has either served his term or been pardoned or perhaps even escaped from custody. He could be a dangerous character — resentful and vengeful if tackled in the wrong way.' He paused to let the force of his argument sink in. Mr Weatherby looked worried. 'Has it not occurred to you,' Middleton went on earnestly, 'that such a fellow, with the support of some of your own men, could make off with every animal you possess? Yes, and cut all our throats into the bargain if they had a mind to! Have you thought of that, Henry?'

Weatherby shook his head. It was clear he had not thought of it but was now doing so. 'I'll be guided by you, James,' he said in a subdued voice.

'Then I beg you to let me deal with the fellow. It will come better from me since it is not my land he is occupying.'

'You'll go alone? Is that wise?'

'No, no! You must come with me as a witness but, please, say nothing unless I refer to you.'

'When shall we go?'

'The sooner the better. I'll place Morgan in charge of the camp and we'll be off now.'

Chapter 11

'Indians'

Morgan watched with misgiving as the two men rode off. He wished he could have gone with them for there was no knowing what sort of man the squatter might be or, indeed, if he were alone. One violent man would be bad enough but several might be more than two gentlemen could handle. Thomas sensed his mood. 'Is something wrong, Morgan?' he asked.

Morgan shook his head, smiling. 'Not that I know of, boyo,' he replied lightly, 'but there might well be if you and your sister don't keep Mistress McInnes's cooking fire well provided with sticks. Away you go now. Take your sister. There be plenty of dry wood lying under those trees.'

The trees Morgan had indicated filled a shallow gully running down to the river. The ground beneath them, undisturbed since time began, was soft and spongy with centuries of rotted bark and leaves. Brother and sister worked in silence, gathering up the lighter of the dead branches that lay about in profusion.

'I wonder what happened to that boy?' Thomas asked suddenly.

His sister's nose wrinkled with distaste. 'You mean that ... that dirty little urchin?'

'He couldn't have gone back across that flooded river and he wouldn't dare show himself at Major Murdoch's place. He must be getting terribly hungry by now...' He turned quickly as he heard Prudence's bundle of sticks clatter to the ground. She was standing bolt upright, hands over her mouth, staring with wide, frightened eyes into a dense grove of trees.

'Pru! What's the matter?' he exclaimed in alarm.

'Look!' she managed to gasp in a scarcely audible whisper.

Thomas stared in the direction of her shaking finger but could see only tree trunks, solid and still as stone pillars. Then, in the corner of his eye, he caught a slight movement. He swung around and a thrill of fear ran through him. Half hidden in the dappled shadows stood a tall naked black man, a bundle of long, thin spears in one hand and a curiously shaped club in the other. Then he made out another still form... and another... and another. He sensed there were many more, unseen, staring; he could feel their eyes upon him from all sides.

'Don't be afraid,' he said, his mouth suddenly dry. 'Morgan says they are quite harmless if we don't upset them.'

'Why are they carrying spears then?' Prudence whispered.

As he recovered from his first fright, Thomas realised that had the silent watchers meant mischief they could have attacked before either Prudence or he had been aware of their presence. 'They're only hunting, I expect,' he said, some confidence returning. 'Perhaps they've never seen white people before.'

Prudence swallowed nervously. 'What shall we do? We can't stand here for ever.'

Thomas's inclination was to make a bolt for it but he was not sure what effect this might have on the silent watchers. The problem was solved by a mocking voice behind them. 'Ye're feared, ain't ye?'

They swung around together to face Maggie Jackson's kid, his naked body so darkened by exposure to the sun as to be almost as invisible in the shadows of the trees as the Aborigines themselves.

'You!' cried Thomas delightedly. 'Are you with them?'

Suddenly conscious of the boy's nudity, Prudence turned her back on him. 'Oh, you are shocking!' she declared in a horrified voice.

The kid's laugh rang out loud and derisive. 'Wearing duds don't mean nothink. Only whites cover 'emselves up. Blacks got more bloody sense. They got no duds — nor no jails, nor no so'jers and no floggings, neither. The blacks is better than your mob any day!'

Prudence stood with her back turned resolutely to the voice but Thomas was less concerned with appearances; to him the boy, naked or clothed, was a friend in need. 'Help us get away,' he pleaded. 'Tell us what to do, please.'

'They won't hurt ye. Just dance, that's all ye got to do.'

'Dance?' Thomas repeated. 'Why?'

'Make 'em laugh. They never seen no whites close to before.'

Thomas looked at his sister's bloodless face and back to the kid's unashamed, grinning nakedness. Was he trying to make fools of them? 'If we dance out of the woods, will you come with us?' he asked.

'Thomas!' his sister protested. 'He's... he's...' She couldn't force herself to say the word.

The grin had slipped from the kid's face. 'Come with you? Not bloody likely! They reckon I lifted them sparklers from your old woman but I never! Youse lot can go to hell!'

'But that was a mistake,' Thomas assured him. 'Dr Middleton found all Mama's jewellery hidden in Jake Brightwell's tobacco pouch.'

A shrewd, self-satisfied smile replaced the kid's angry frown. His white teeth seemed to shine out from between his grimy cheeks. 'Yeh?' he said in a pleased voice. 'How'd he find out then?'

'I don't know,' Thomas replied. 'I think it was just lucky.'

'Thomas!' wailed Prudence, over her shoulder. 'Tell him to send those dreadful creatures away so we can go home.'

'I can't tell 'em what to do,' the kid answered her. 'I can tell you, but. Dance! Go on! They won't hurt ye!'

'You come with us,' Thomas begged. 'You'll be quite safe now. We're your friends.'

'The blacks is my friends,' the kid stated simply.

Suddenly a new voice broke the silence. 'Thomas! Miss Prudence!' Morgan called from beyond the trees. 'Where are you?' A wave of relief swept over them as they heard the cracking of dry sticks under Morgan's feet as he approached. 'You've been long enough gathering them few sticks,' he observed, looking at the meagre bundle Thomas was still clutching to him. 'Mistress McInnes is waiting for her kindling.'

'Oh, Morgan!' Prudence cried, all sense of their social difference forgotten. 'Save us from these dreadful creatures, please!'

Morgan looked around him quickly. He saw only the sturdy, impassive columns of the eucalypts.

'They've gone!' Thomas exclaimed in astonishment.

'Who's gone?' Morgan asked.

'The black men!' the boy replied, his eyes searching the now empty bush. 'We were afraid to run away because they had spears and clubs. Maggie Jackson's kid told us to dance.'

'So he was with them, was he?'

'He was indeed!' declared Prudence. 'I was never so ashamed in my life!'

'He had no clothes on,' Thomas explained. 'Not a stitch! None of them did.'

Morgan fought against a smile as he stooped to pick up the bundle of firewood Prudence had dropped. She stalked primly ahead, empty handed. They walked in silence until the trees were left behind and they were in sight of the camp. Then Morgan spoke. 'If you'll take my advice, you'll not mention the Indians to your mam. They're harmless enough, look you. They all ran away when they heard me coming so they can't be so fearsome, now can they? But the thought of them so close will frighten your mam, I shouldn't wonder, and she's fretting in her mind as it is over that squatter fellow.'

Chapter 12

Confrontation

The meeting with the squatter started off amicably enough. Dr Middleton dismounted and greeted him politely. 'Good day to you, my friend!'

The man's first words revealed his Irish background. 'And good day to your two selves, sir. What might ye two gentlemen be doing in this far-off place?'

The doctor ignored the question. 'My name is Middleton. James Middleton. I am a surgeon. This is my friend, Henry Weatherby.'

'Me own name is Reilly — Michael Joseph Reilly.' The man extended a calloused hand but there was a certain wariness in his manner.

'I expect you find it rather lonely away up here on your own,' the doctor said as they shook hands. 'I take it you are alone?'

'Aye, to be sure! There's nought but me own self and the sheep and a tribe of blacks in this whole country as far as the eye can see and beyond.'

'Do you find the blacks hereabouts friendly, Mr Reilly? I've heard they can be troublesome where there are sheep. They regard all animals as fair game for their spears, so I'm told.'

Reilly appeared to hesitate for a moment. 'The blacks don't give me no trouble,' he said.

'Have you been long in these parts, Mr Reilly?' Middleton went on casually.

The man regarded him with mounting distrust. 'Long enough to raise up this flock of sheep ye see about ye now.' He paused, thinking. 'Fourteen years I had Guv'mint business to attend to then, when me contrack with the Crown was up, I made me way across country to this spot with a handful of them critters. Six years past that was, as best a man can keep count of the time with no church bells to remind him of the Sabbath.'

'James,' said Mr Weatherby impatiently, 'I think we had best come to the crux of the matter.'

'Yes, perhaps you're right, Henry.' Middleton faced the squatter. 'You must have realised, Mr Reilly, that this is not entirely a social visit. There is business to be discussed. It concerns this land you have been using...'

The Irishman's face clouded, his eyes narrowed and his manner changed to undisguised hostility. 'So that's the way of it, eh? It's me own land ye're after, is it?'

'Not *your* land, my man... *mine*.' Weatherby corrected him sternly.

The doctor raised a warning hand. 'If you please, Henry,' he frowned. 'Allow me to handle this. I'm quite sure we can come to a friendly arrangement with Mr Reilly.'

The squatter's blood was up. 'Cut the fancy patter, damn ye!' he cried angrily. 'These are me own sheep and, by the same token, it's me own land they're grazing by right of long usage. I done nothin' agin the law. Nothin', ye hear me?'

'No one is questioning your ownership of the sheep,' Middleton assured him, 'nor suggesting that you have broken the law. Up to this moment you had every right to graze your sheep on this land. But now, unfortunately, the circumstances have changed.'

'Who says so?' the squatter challenged him.

'I do,' Middleton replied evenly, 'as a Justice of the Peace on behalf of the Governor of New South Wales who has formally granted two thousand acres hereabouts to this gentleman who has the deed of covenant to prove it.'

'So it's a piece of paper ye have, is it?' the Irishman sneered. 'Then tell me, if ye will, what makes ye so sure this wild land is the land spoken of in the deed for I've seen no surveyors around lately at all.'

'You should know how it's done, Mr Reilly. An official land grant is first described in the deed as closely as possible and the formal survey is carried out later.'

'Aye, I know well enough how it's done!' Reilly responded bitterly. 'It was bloody English swells the likes of yer two selves took the land from under me own feet back home in Ireland, so it was! Now ye follow me all the way up here to the backside of nowhere and think to snatch the land from me again! Well, damn yer eyes, I'll not be moved and that's me last word!'

'It's quite impossible to reason with the fellow,' Weatherby remarked tactlessly.

Reilly turned on him furiously. 'Impossible, is it? Now that's the first true word to pass yer lips since ye come here. Try moving me off me own land and ye'll find the truth of it for yerself!'

'In that case,' Weatherby declared, 'I shall have no alternative but to call upon the military to move you off by force.'

The squatter spat contemptuously. 'So'jers! 'Way up here? It's a simple-minded man ye must be surely to put yer trust in so'jers and them so far away!'

'Please listen to me,' the doctor said soothingly, his patience sustained by sympathy for the man's plight and desire for a peaceful settlement. 'What we are here to tell you is that, in the course of time, Mr Weatherby will need to take over this land for his animals and I myself shall be moving further on to take over another two thousand acres higher up the river. Sooner or later you will have to find other grazing for your flock but neither of us is so unreasonable as to expect you to move at once.'

Reason and fairness were lost on the angry man. 'Move on, is it?' he shouted, making Weatherby's horse rear up and nearly unseat him. 'After six long years, drought and flood, and me the man who opened up this land even before the murdering major himself fouled the soil of it by setting his foot upon it, God rot him!'

'You would do well to keep a civil tongue in your head when speaking of your betters,' Weatherby admonished him coldly.

Such an ill-timed remark was the last straw. Reilly's right hand slid inside the loose folds of his homemade jute shirt and came out holding a stubby, singleshot pistol of ancient design. Middleton took a step backwards in his surprise. A flintlock, he noted instinctively, probably poorly primed and with an even chance of misfiring but quite capable of killing a man at close range. 'It would be very foolish of you to use that, Mr Reilly,' he said quietly. 'We are unarmed and if you were even to wound one of us you would be a wanted man with a price on your head. You said you'd served your term so that makes you as free a man as either of us.'

'Ah, to be sure, so I did!' The man's rage seemed to have melted into an almost genial mockery with the gun giving him the upper hand. 'A free man the like of yerselves, am I now? Well, if you was me you'd know yerself for a liar. I'll tell ye the great difference between the likes of you and me. If I was free and equal to yerselves, ye'd not be after hounding me off me own land. Ye'd not be minding me past life, whether I was living like a martyred saint or a murdering blaggard in a red tunic with me heart full of bloody deeds and me breast hung with gaudy ribbons to prove it! That's what it is, surely!'

He paused for breath, the pistol still pointing at the doctor while his eyes flitted from one man to the other, judging the effect of his words. His bitterness had returned in full flood and he was shouting again. He waved his pistol threateningly. 'Be off with ye now before I forget I'm a free man the same as yerselves and destroy one or other of ye!'

Dr Middleton lifted himself into the saddle with unhurried dignity. 'I'm sorry you've taken this attitude, Mr Reilly,' he said as he turned his horse's head. 'I can only hope your better judgement will prevail when you think the matter over. If not, I'm afraid you'll have to take the consequences.'

'I ain't afraid of yer murdering redcoats!' the squatter called after them. 'See ye keep off my land or, by all the saints, I'll get ye.' He lowered his pistol slowly. 'And if I don't get ye,' he shouted, 'I'll see the blacks do, d'ye hear me?'

Chapter 13

Robin Adair

By the time the two men returned to camp they had discussed the problem of the squatter from every angle without finding a solution.

'Then what in heaven's name are we to do?' Mr Weatherby wanted to know. 'Surely you don't think we should just give in to the scoundrel?'

'Certainly not!'

'Then what do you propose?'

'That we ignore the fellow for the time being and I believe that when he sees we have every intention of staying here he will move on of his own accord.'

Weatherby was far from convinced. 'And what do you suppose he meant by saying that if he didn't get us, he would make sure the Indians did?'

'That, I confess, troubles me a little,' the doctor replied thoughtfully. 'It may be no more than empty bluster but it is a possibility we cannot afford to overlook.'

Dr Middleton was more concerned about the chances of trouble with the Aborigines than he cared to admit. As soon as they got back to camp, he took Morgan aside and described the meeting to him. The Welshman stroked his curly beard. 'Now there's a churlish fellow for you,' he remarked as the doctor ended. 'But it's all my eye and Betty Martin about the Indians if you ask me, sir. It doesn't seem likely they're a dangerous lot hereabouts, look you.'

Middleton looked surprised. 'What makes you say that? Have you seen any of them about lately?'

'No, sir, not me. But Thomas and Miss Prudence have.' Morgan related what he knew of the encounter with the Aborigines.

'And that boy was with them, you say?'

'Aye, sir. Running wild and naked as the day he was born, from their account of it.'

The doctor's expression brightened. 'Ah, then perhaps with his help we may be able to make friends with them...' He broke off, his hopes checked by a problem. 'But first we must find him.'

'There's one person as might flush him out,' Morgan suggested diffidently. His ruddy cheeks heightened in colour and he looked away as he spoke. 'Mistress McInnes it was I had in mind, sir.'

' What makes you think she could do it?'

'When the lad wanted to tell someone he could trust about Jake stealing the jewels, who did he go to? Not me. Not you, sir. It was to her he turned, look you.'

'That's true,' the doctor remarked thoughtfully.

'She's a fine, motherly young woman, sir, is Mistress McInnes,' Morgan went on earnestly and, for the first time, Middleton noticed the revealing rosiness of his cheeks and the eagerness in his voice. 'She's a woman any man could take to, let alone a poor motherless waif like him. She reminds him of his own mam, I shouldn't wonder...'

The doctor's lips twitched. 'I see what you mean,' he responded gravely. 'But I can't very well send the girl out into the bush to look for him, especially if he's living with the blacks.'

'No need for that, sir, from what the children told me. She won't need to find him, look you, for he'll find her, just like he did Thomas and the girl.'

The doctor nodded understandingly. 'Very well. Leave it to me.'

The plan was simple. After dark they should be able to locate the Aboriginal camp by the light of its fires. Since Mrs Weatherby would have retired for the night, Mandy would be free to help and could approach the camp, with Morgan and Dr Middleton keeping out of sight unless needed. To attract the boy's attention, Mandy would sing. How the Aborigines would react to the sound of a white woman singing near their camp in the dead of night they could only guess. It could be dangerous and the doctor was worried. 'Are you sure you want to do this, Mandy?' he asked her anxiously.

'I'm not afraid, sir,' she lied with a reassuring smile.

When it was dark and the Weatherbys had gone to bed, Morgan and the doctor slipped away with Mandy. They skirted the trees among which Thomas and Prudence had seen the Aborigines and there below them the small, scattered fires of the native camp twinkled like a tiny constellation that had strayed into the blackness of the river valley. Mandy stumbled over the rough ground but the quickening of her heart was not entirely the result of exertion. The sullen, impoverished appearance of the blacks she had seen in Sydney and Parramatta did not make her feel they could have any love for the white folk nor, from what she had observed from their treatment, any reason to trust or respect them. And two muskets, she well knew, would be no match for a shower of spears.

As they neared the camp the only sounds that drifted to them on the light breeze were occasional bursts of infectious laughter. Mandy had never heard Aboriginal people laugh before. It was a comforting and encouraging sound.

'Sing when you are ready, Mandy,' the doctor said. 'We'll be close behind you.' The two men waited as Mandy rustled off through the long, coarse grass to get closer to the fires flickering between the trees on the river flat. They moved stealthily after her as she began to hum, a little tremulously at first, an ancient Gaelic melody. She had a sweet and true voice and, as she gained confidence, the words the Scottish poet, Robert Burns, had written for the old tune floated back to them.

> What's this dull town to me?
> Robin's not near.
> What was't I wished to see.
> What wished to hear?
> Where all the joy and mirth
> Made this town heav'n on earth?
> Och, they're all fled with thee,
>   Robin Adair...

The lilting tune stopped. The two men crouched, ears straining. No laughter came from the camp now.

Mandy's voice rose again, further away. The watchers slipped noiselessly after her. The song continued, made more haunting by the darkness and the alien surroundings...

> Yet he I loved so well
> Still in my heart shall dwell.
> Och, I can ne'er forget
>   Robin Adair...

A boyish voice, shrill with anger, shattered the silence. 'Stow that, damn ye!'

Morgan and the doctor watched, muskets cocked. Their eyes had become accustomed to the dim glow from the native fires and they could just make out the scene: Mandy motionless beside the black bole of a tree and the kid, leaping wildly over a campfire as he raced straight for her.

'What the hell youse doing here?' they heard him shout as he confronted her. 'Ye must be glocky, coming here in the dark all by yerself!' He went on quickly before Mandy could speak, the anger in his voice tempered by curiosity. 'And how'd ye come by what ye was singing? Who learned it ye?'

'Everyone knows it,' Mandy replied calmly. 'It's a Scottish song.'

The boy stared at her suspiciously but his aggressive manner had softened a little. 'Don't you never sing it again, see?' he ordered her sternly.

'Why not?' Mandy retorted. 'It's a lovely song to be sure and I'll sing it as I please. Do ye no' like the song, then?'

'Never ye mind!'

Mandy bristled. 'Don't ye dare speak to me in that fashion, laddie,' she reprimanded him sharply, 'or I'll tan the backside of ye, big and all as ye are.'

75

The boy suddenly became aware of his nakedness. He half turned away uncomfortably. Mandy unpinned her long cape and held it out to him, smiling. He snatched it from her ungraciously and wrapped it around himself.

'Got yerself lost, did ye?' he asked mockingly.

'No. I came looking for you.'

The boy was nonplussed for a moment. 'What for? Ye knows I never lifted them luggers of the old woman's. It was Jake nailed'em, like I telled ye.'

'Not about that. It's the doctor and Morgan Jones need your help.'

'To hell with 'em!' the boy exclaimed. 'They reckoned it was me snatched them sparklers. I ain't going to help 'em.'

'It would be helping me, too, laddie. Will ye no' come back with me and talk with the doctor?' she pleaded.

He appeared to consider the idea. 'If I comes with ye,' he said at last, 'I sleeps in your tent with you of a night.' Mandy hesitated. She had been prepared for him to make conditions but this was totally unexpected. What would Mrs Weatherby say? That was a silly question, she reflected swiftly; she knew only too well what Mrs Weatherby would say.

'I'm not sure I've the power to promise ye such a thing,' she replied gravely. 'It might not be thought fitting.'

'Then I ain't coming!' he replied with finality. He turned away, stripping the cape from his shoulders, but Mandy stopped him.

'Wait,' she said. 'I'll ask the doctor. If he's agreeable, it'll be possible, I'm sure.'

'I'll come for youse, not for him, mind', the boy warned her.

'That's understood then,' Mandy agreed. 'But there will have to be other things understood if you're to share my tent. When your mother was alive, did she no' teach ye to be clean and sweet smelling?'

His face clouded. 'What d'youse know of my mam?' he demanded, the old antagonism returning. 'She never did nothing wrong or bad, my mam. It's all bloody lies, see?' He glared at Mandy challengingly.

'All I ever heard tell of your mam,' she replied calmly, 'is that she was a beautiful young woman who kept to herself and was sorely tried by others.'

The gentle, unexpected response, delivered with such quiet sincerity, disarmed the boy completely. He stood staring into her face, his lips moving soundlessly as though trying to find words to express the disturbing emotions that struggled within him. Mandy returned his gaze steadily. Her voice was soft and understanding as she said, 'Your mam used to sing that song, did she no'?' He nodded, his eyes brimming with tears. 'It was you was her own Robin, eh?'

The boy's chin trembled uncontrollably. Unable to speak, he nodded again, making the tears overflow down his grubby cheeks. Suddenly he gave a hoarse, choking sob and, to the amazement of the two men watching, threw his arms around Mandy and buried his face in her breast. Mandy held him tightly to her, rocking gently till the shaking of his shoulders and the harsh, gasping sounds of his weeping subsided. Then she pushed

77

him gently away, holding him at arm's length and smiling into his face made tragically comic by the white tear tracks in the grime.

'Dinna be ashamed to weep for your mam, laddie,' she said softly. 'A man's no' worth his salt that canna' weep tears once in a while.' The boy managed an uncertain smile. 'Ye'll be *my* Robin from this time on, eh?' Mandy whispered. He nodded, brushing the tears roughly from his eyes and further smearing his cheeks. 'But there's something ye must do before ye share a dwelling of mine,' she went on, her face wrinkling in mock distaste, 'and that's scrub yerself in the river for when ye're with me ye'll no' need to blacken yourself to look like an Indian.'

The boy's laugh rang out. The men saw him turn and call cheerful words of explanation and assurance to his unseen Aboriginal friends then, taking Mandy's hand, walk confidently beside her in their direction. He stopped abruptly when the two men rose from the long grass with their muskets.

'It's no' but Dr Middleton and Mr Jones,' Mandy explained as he hung back uncertainly. 'They followed to make sure I came to no harm.'

'There's nothing to fear now, lad. We're your friends,' the doctor assured him.

'I promised I would take care of him,' Mandy went on. 'Even to sharing my tent with him. Goodness only knows what Mrs Weatherby will say!'

'Leave that lady to me,' Middleton said with quiet confidence. 'You did well, Mandy. Thank you.'

The girl smiled. 'And from this night the wee man has a name. He'll answer to "Rob", will ye no', Rob?'

The boy muttered agreement. It was clear he resented the presence of the men. Morgan gazed uneasily into the surrounding shadows. 'We should be taking ourselves back to the camp before the blacks find us,' he said.

'The blacks won't do ye no hurt,' Rob growled. 'They never hurt no one as doesn't hurt them. Not like whites.'

'Then while we're down here close to the river,' Mandy said matter-of-factly, 'Ye can wash the dirt off yerself. Mr Jones will give ye a hand if ye ask him civilly.'

'I don't want no help,' the boy answered gruffly.

He slipped Mandy's cape from his shoulders, tossed it to her and disappeared. A few moments later a mighty splashing, punctuated by much snorting, coughing and spitting, came from the direction of the dark river.

Chapter 14

The Currency Lad

Half an hour later in the sleeping camp, Rob, wrapped in a blanket, was crouched beside the fire tucking into a plate of hot stew which Mandy had put aside in the hope of his return. She scraped the last of it from the black iron pot and ladled it on to his plate. The boy looked up at her gratefully, cheeks bulging.

'Real good scran,' he mumbled, then, patting his stomach, 'a proper tightener!'

Morgan regarded him thoughtfully over a mug of steaming tea. 'We'll have to find some clothes for him now that he's given away all his old duds to the Indians.'

'Just as well,' Mandy said. 'They were no' but rags.'

'He shall be freshly outfitted from the supply wagon first thing in the morning,' the doctor told them. 'Though I doubt there will be anything to fit him'.

Mandy finished scouring the stew pot and hung it upside down on a stake near the fire. 'I'll cut them down to fit him,' she said.

The doctor pulled out his watch and gave it a quick glance. 'It's after midnight, Mandy. High time you were in bed.'

Rob stood up to follow her. 'Wait awhile, Rob,' Middleton said. 'I want to ask you a few questions. It won't take long, then you can curl up in your blanket before Mandy's tent and make sure no one disturbs her for the rest of the night.'

'She said I'd kip inside with her,' the boy reminded him.

'Of course, on a wet night, if you keep yourself in her good books, she'll not mind, I'm sure. But you don't strike me as an inside sort of fellow, not like Thomas. You're more like Morgan here who sleeps under a wagon in any sort of weather.'

Rob sat down again, flattered by the comparison with the big blacksmith. 'What ye want then?' he asked with casual condescension.

'First of all, how well do you know these natives?'

'I lived with 'em, didn't I? I knowed I can trust 'em. More'n I can say of whites.'

'Then you must be able to speak their language?'

'I vokers their patter and they vokers me good enough.'

'Would you say they are friendly towards us?'

'They got nothink agin ye — not yet.'

The doctor frowned. 'What do you mean by "not yet"?'

'What ye going to do when they spears a sheep then?' the boy countered.

81

'Why should they need to kill a sheep? There are surely more than enough kangaroos and other animals for them.'

'Sheep is animals like the rest, ain't they?' the boy argued. 'Youse whites shoot kangaroos and them things, don't ye? So why not blacks spear a sheep for a change of tucker?'

'But kangaroos are wild creatures, look you,' Morgan reasoned. 'Not like sheep.'

'Nevertheless there is justice in what the lad says,' the doctor remarked.

Sensing an unexpected sympathy for his Aboriginal friends, Rob jumped to his feet and faced the doctor. With a sweeping gesture he indicated the surrounding darkness. 'Now all this here land,' he began vehemently, 'it was all theirs till youse lot come along and vamped it off of 'em. It was youse lot brought all these here cows and sheep and horses to eat all the tucker down. The kangaroos and them things ain't glocky. When they got no tucker left they moves away somewheres else where there's more tucker for 'em, see ...?'

'And a good thing, too, if you ask me,' Morgan said. 'Then the Indians will follow them.'

'The blacks can't move off of their own land and go and live on land that ain't theirs', Rob explained impatiently. 'They'd get 'emselves killed!'

Middleton looked worried. 'So what you're telling us is that if our animals drive the wild ones away, the natives will hunt our stock and consider it their right to do so?'

'It's their land ye're sitting on, ain't it?' was the simple reply. 'It was youse lot what vamped it off of 'em.'

'What the lad says is quite true', the doctor agreed reluctantly with the air of a man not enjoying a struggle with a troubled conscience. 'The land is theirs by right of long occupation and, not to mince words on the matter, we are stealing it from them.'

'But the Indians make no good use of the land, look you,' Morgan protested earnestly. 'Surely to goodness it's best we should take the good land and show them how to clear it and grow wheat and barley and raise sheep and cattle on it instead of letting it go to waste, isn't it?'

The boy turned on him furiously. 'Youse don't know nothink!' he exclaimed. 'The land and them trees and the animals is all they got and you got no call to vamp it off of 'em!'

In the softly flickering orange light of the dying fire, Morgan turned to Middleton helplessly, expecting support for what to him was the only sensible way to look at the problem. 'That's what the government in London sent the first ships here for, look you.'

'No, Morgan,' the doctor answered firmly. 'The lad is right and you and I are both wrong. The orders given to Captain Cook when he was sent to explore the great unknown southern ocean were quite the opposite. He was given to understand in no uncertain terms by the Admiralty and the Royal Society that "the natives are the natural and the legal possessors of the regions they inhabit and no European nation has the right to occupy their country or settle on it without their free consent..." So you see, Morgan, you and I are both breaking the rules with the government's blessing.' Rob nodded complacently. The actual words had meant little to him but the doctor's tone and Morgan's obvious bewilderment and discomfiture told him all he need to know. 'This is a problem to test the wisdom of Solomon himself,' the doctor continued thoughtfully. 'Yet it's important we should befriend these people and earn their trust and cooperation.' He looked at Rob hopefully. 'Tell me, lad have you heard of a man named Reilly in these parts?'

'Reilly? He's an old lag. Been up here a long time. He don't give 'em no trouble.'

'Would you think he was friendly with the blacks?'

'My oath!' Rob retorted with a grin. 'He dabs it up with one of the black women, name of Wiumbeen. They got two kids.'

The doctor closed his eyes and slowly lowered his head into his hands.

Morgan looked at him in despair. 'Now there's a poser, indeed to goodness!' he said, shaking his head. 'I don't see how we're going to trump that, sir!'

'Let's get to bed,' Middleton said wearily. 'We've done enough for one day. Sleep clears the mind wonderfully.'

Next morning, as Prudence and her brother were seated at breakfast, a strange sight met their astonished gaze. Staggering up from the creek with a pail of water in each hand came a youthful figure clad only in a baggy pair of coarse canvas trousers, the waist gathered into folds and the legs rolled up to the knees. They watched as the pails were delivered to Mandy at the campfire.

'I do believe it's Maggie Jackson's kid!' Thomas exclaimed.

His sister stared at the stranger's sun-tanned body. 'Never!' she declared. 'He's so clean.'

'Let's go and find out then,' Thomas said, jumping up eagerly and running across to where Rob was trimming kindling wood with a small axe. His sister followed at a more dignified pace.

'Hello!' Thomas greeted the stranger a little uncertainly. 'You're Maggie Jackson's kid, aren't you?'

Rob, unaware of his wonderfully changed appearance, looked up from his work. 'Youse gone blind or summat?' he enquired with heavy sarcasm.

Prudence looked him up and down haughtily. 'What are you doing here?'

'Making meself useful,' Rob retorted. 'More'n you lot ever done.' As an afterthought he nodded towards Mandy, bending over the fire. 'For her, see? Not for nobody else. I'm free, I am. I'm currency.'

'What do you mean by "currency"?' Thomas asked.

'Currency is when ye're born here. Free.' With a scornful nod he indicated the convicts, packing the wagons for the day's journey. 'Not like them canaries as come out under hatches. Not like youse bloody illegitimates, neither.' He gave a derisive snort. 'Ye can't gull me with yer square-rigging and yer flash patter. Currency's better than any of youse lot. Ye're scum alongside of me!'

At the sheer audacity of this last claim, Prudence gasped. 'How dare you say such a thing!' she rebuked him angrily. 'I'll have you know that our father is the son of a baronet — the late Sir George Weatherby! We can trace our family tree back to William the Conqueror...' Her voice trailed off uncertainly as she saw Mandy approaching.

'All of us can trace our forebears back to Adam and Eve if we've a mind to,' Mandy remarked as she gathered up an armful of the firewood Rob had prepared for her. 'Now, come along, Rob, and start packing for me. We've got to be on the road again as soon as I've got Mrs Weatherby dressed.'

'Rob?' Thomas repeated in surprise. 'Is that his real name?'

'Aye, it is that,' Mandy replied firmly over her shoulder. 'Rob is the laddie's name and that is what ye'll kindly call him by from now on.'

Mr Weatherby had undertaken to explain to his wife the necessity for Rob's presence but to obtain her consent to his attachment to Mandy was, he knew, going to be a test of diplomacy.

Mrs Weatherby had exploded when the case had been outlined to her. 'How can that wretched child possibly protect our beasts from the natives? If they steal from us it is our duty to punish them. The Indians should be kept in their place, by force if needs be, as they are in other colonies.'

'The nub of the matter is, m'dear, that it will save a great deal of trouble if we can keep on good terms with them and this is where the boy comes in, d'you see? He is already friendly with them and can speak their language. He can be our ambassador, as it were, d'you follow, m'dear?'

'Ambassador indeed!' Mrs Weatherby declared. 'The solution is quite simple to my mind; if the natives become troublesome they must be taught a sharp lesson. Their spears are no match for our muskets, I imagine.'

'Alas, according to the law of the land,' her husband replied wearily, 'it is just as serious a crime to kill a black man as a white man. But we don't want any bloodshed if it can be avoided.'

A shadow fell on the tent. 'Ah, come in, James!' Weatherby called, relieved to have an ally. 'I was just telling Mrs Weatherby of the unfortunate necessity for that boy's presence with us and was about to mention his attachment to McInnes...'

'McInnes?' his wife interrupted sharply. 'How do you propose to involve her, may I ask?'

The doctor took up the explanation as Weatherby had hoped. 'Mandy McInnes is the only person the lad trusts. He made it a condition of his return that he should be answerable only to her.'

'McInnes is my personal maid and I will not share her. Certainly not with that dreadful little ruffian!'

Middleton regarded her with undisguised impatience. 'This could well be a desperate situation, m'am; more desperate than you realise. Mandy McInnes is the only one who can keep the boy with us and keep him we must in the meantime.' He paused then went on firmly. 'I am well aware that there are topics on which we do not see eye to eye, m'am, but on this one there can be no compromise'.

Mrs Weatherby smoothed the lacy bodice of her gown. 'You are certainly right there, sir. However, I can see that in this instance I must bow to your demands.'

'Not demands, m'am. Advice,' he corrected her.

Chapter 15

Warning

Working with Mandy, Rob seemed to have become a reformed character. He applied himself devotedly to Mandy's service and pointedly avoided unnecessary contact with the Weatherby children. He helped her erect her tent, cut a vast quantity of dry grass for her bed and then filled a large copper boiler with water from the river and kept a fire roaring beneath it while Mandy attended to the laundry which had accumulated on the journey. It was later, during the wringing, that the trouble started. Rob had been astonished at the strength in Mandy's slim wrists as he gripped one end of a sheet and she twisted the other, causing cascades of water to gush from its folds. Only with great difficulty was he able to hang on to his end.

'Don't you let go now!' Mandy warned him. 'You drop it in the dirt after all my hard work and I'll box your ears!'

Rob laughed. He was so intent on his task that he didn't notice Dr Middleton and Morgan until the doctor spoke.

'You've a willing worker here, I see, Mandy.'

'Aye, to be sure, sir,' the girl replied cheerfully. 'And it's no' light work for the laddie, either.'

Without a word, Morgan stepped forward and his two brawny blacksmith's hands closed over Rob's end of the sheet now twisted tight as a ship's hawser.

The boy turned on him savagely. 'Let go, damn ye!' he shouted, taking one hand from the sheet to strike at Morgan.

Startled, Morgan stepped back and the sheet spun from Rob's hand, spreading itself on the muddy ground.

The boy's eyes blazed. 'Now look what ye done, ye glocky fool!' he flared at Morgan.

In the embarrassed silence that followed, Rob stared at Mandy. 'It was him done it, not me,' he said, sullen and defiant. The forlorn hope flashed through his mind that if Mandy were disposed to box ears, Morgan might be the one to suffer.

Her reaction surprised him. ''Tis no great misfortune,' she remarked mildly. 'I'll give it another rinse while ye beg Mr Jones's pardon for your rudeness, ye hear me, Rob?' She gathered up the muddied sheet and made for the river bank while Rob glared at the Welshman who returned his stare coldly.

'Mandy is right, Rob,' the doctor said. 'You owe Morgan an apology.'

The boy looked at the ground. 'He shoved hisself in,' he growled in a surly voice.

'Those are not the words that have to be said. The words are, "I'm sorry, Morgan". Now come along, Rob. Let's hear them.'

The boy knew he was cornered. He wanted to run away and never come back yet from some dark, long-forgotten corner of his troubled mind came a dim vision of another young woman who had chided him in moments of childish tantrums. Tears welled into his eyes. He clamped his jaws tight shut and screwed his forehead into a scowl to prevent the tears from showing as he continued to stare at the ground. 'Sorry,' he muttered from between clenched teeth.

'There, Morgan,' the doctor said approvingly. 'An apology, if somewhat brief.'

'Aye, sir,' the big man replied. 'And took in the spirit it were given.'

'Well, now that's settled, Rob, perhaps you and I and Morgan could continue the talk we were having last night? There's a lot more we want to learn about your black friends.'

The boy looked down to the river where Mandy was rinsing the heavy, water-logged sheet with difficulty. 'I got to help her first,' he said, his old independent spirit returning. 'I'll talk to youse after.'

They watched him run to join Mandy and nod his head in answer to a question. Evidently she was satisfied for she handed him one end of the sheet and together they struggled with it.

The doctor turned to his companion. 'You think I'm too lenient with the lad, don't you, Morgan?'

The Welshman shook his head. 'It's not my place to say, sir, but I tell you what — if he was mine now I'd warm his backside for him!'

The doctor swallowed a smile. 'I know how you feel but the lad's too high-spirited, too independent for that treatment. If he's ever to be tamed and made fit for civilised society there is only one person with the necessary patience and understanding — and that person is Mandy.'

'I can believe that, sir,' Morgan agreed, warming at once to his favourite subject.

'You admire her greatly, don't you?' the doctor said. Morgan looked away in confusion at the directness of the question. 'Then take my advice, man,' Middleton went on. 'Make sure you and the boy don't end up rivals for her attention. Your cause could be set back if she had to choose between you. Believe me, a big, strapping fellow like you has little chance against a helpless waif like Rob.'

Morgan pondered this paradox. Then his usual good humour returned and he grinned at the doctor. 'I wouldn't call that boyo helpless now, would you?'

On a smooth rock ledge beside the river, Mandy and Rob were again tackling the heavy job of wringing. The sound of their laughter floated back to the two men. Suddenly their attention was diverted from the river by a hoarse cry from behind them. They turned to see Jake stumbling towards them, the limp body of a sheep slung across his shoulders. They hurried to meet him and stared blankly at the carcass he dumped at their feet.

'What's this, Jake?' the doctor asked.

'Dead!' he gasped. 'Stone dead! I brung her straight away to show ye.'

Jake turned the animal's head over with his foot. On the underside of the neck the wool was stained red. Morgan parted the strands of wool to reveal a small, deep wound. 'Speared in the neck, mister, see?' the convict said, still breathing hard. 'It was them blacks done it!'

Middleton looked away, troubled. Jake glanced from one to the other, awaiting an explanation.

'If they'd wanted the animal for food they'd have cut it up,' Middleton said. 'Their leaving it for us to find makes it look like an act of defiance... a challenge.'

'Now why should they want to do such a thing?' Morgan asked. 'There's no one has so much as clapped eyes on an Indian, save for the children, look you. What injury could we have done to them?'

'That is what worries me,' the doctor replied. 'Since we have done them no harm they must have been stirred up against us by someone who does bear us a grudge.' He glanced meaningly at Morgan.

'That there kid was with 'em, mister,' Jake put in eagerly. 'Maggie Jackson's kid, he was living with 'em. It was him put 'em up to it, mark me!' The three men looked to where Mandy and Rob were standing side by side, admiring their handiwork as it flapped, gleaming white, from a rope clothes line strung between two trees and supported in the middle by a sturdy prop, cut and trimmed by Rob.

Middleton turned to the convict. 'The boy had nothing to do with it,' he stated firmly. 'I'll vouch for him. Remember that, Jake.'

Chapter 16

Corroboree

In the velvet darkness of the night, Mrs Weatherby lay uneasily awake, listening to the soft stirring of the breeze outside her tent. Whether it was the restless rustling of leaves that had roused her or the mindless tapping of a loose guy rope she could not decide. These were sounds she had become well used to at night. There was something else... The light wind dropped and, as the silence of the wilderness enclosed her, she held her breath, listening. Suddenly she caught the unusual sound again, faint, murmurous, rhythmical... then a light puff of air carried it off again in a flurry of foliage. She sat up. 'Prudence!' she called quietly.

'What, Mama?' her daughter replied sleepily.

'Ssh! Listen!'

They lay still, hearing only the usual night sounds. 'It's only the wind, Mama,' Prudence said impatiently.

The breeze dropped again and they felt, rather than heard, a far-off drumming, meaningless but strangely menacing. Then the wind washed it away again.

'What was it?' Prudence whispered nervously.

'I don't know but I don't like it. Go and wake your father.'

They gasped as the tent flap was pulled aside and a shadowy form blocked the opening. 'Don't be alarmed,' Mr Weatherby said as he entered and the flap fell into place behind him. 'Did you hear that weird, moaning sound in the distance?'

'Yes, indeed! What do you suppose it might be?'

'I haven't a notion, m'dear, but I've sent Thomas to wake James in case it has some significance.'

When Thomas woke the doctor, he assumed that the boy's mother had been taken ill and rose quickly. Hurriedly thrusting the long tails of his nightshirt into his trousers, he asked for the lady's symptoms.

'It's not Mama,' Thomas explained. 'She and Papa heard a strange noise and they would like you to listen to it, too.'

Middleton sighed. 'What sort of noise?' he asked, trying not to show the annoyance he felt. He stood listening but could hear nothing but the wind so went on dressing with less urgency. They were about to leave the tent when Morgan appeared.

'There's no need for the whole camp to be disturbed,' the doctor assured him. 'Some unusual noise has aroused the Weatherbys, that's all.'

'I heard it,' Morgan said. 'It's the Indians, I shouldn't wonder.'

'Indians?' Middleton was suddenly interested. Morgan glanced sideways at Thomas and nodded.

'Thomas,' the doctor said, 'please go and wake Rob. Tell him I want to speak to him. Then assure your parents there is nothing for them to be concerned about. Tell them to go back to sleep.' He paused. 'And Thomas, no mention of Indians, please.'

'No, sir.' The boy was gone and the two men were left listening.

'I hear it,' Middleton said after a long silence. 'It's the natives, I'm sure. I wonder what it means?' As he spoke a disgruntled Rob appeared. 'What's up?' he grumbled. 'I ain't done nothink.'

'Rob, if you listen carefully...' the doctor began.

'Oh, that!' the boy interrupted. 'I heared 'em. I ain't deaf.'

'The blacks?'

'Course!' His tone was scornful. 'That there's a c'rrob'ree — singing and dancing and that.'

'What does it mean?'

'How the hell do I know? I ain't there, I'm here, ain't I?'

'Is it some kind of war dance, perhaps?' Middleton persisted, trying not to sound anxious.

Rob stood with his head cocked slightly to one side. The men waited for his verdict. 'I dunno,' he responded doubtfully. 'Got to see what's going on and how they got themselves painted up and that.'

'So if you were able to see them you would know whether they were happy or angry or upset about something?' the doctor went on earnestly. 'It's important we should know, Rob.'

'If I seen 'em I reckon I'd granny what they was on about.'

'Would you be prepared to go down to the blacks' camp tonight and find out what this... this c'rrob'ree is about? Morgan and I will go with you.'

'You'll be safe with us, boyo,' Morgan said confidently.

The boy's teeth gleamed white in the candle-light. 'The blacks don't bother me none,' he grinned. 'It ain't no sheep of mine got speared.'

'That's exactly why we need your help, Rob,' Middleton explained. 'You can make them understand that we want to be their friends and that we don't want to drive them away. Later on, when our flocks have increased, if they need meat we'll kill a beast for them. Will you tell them that, Rob?'

Rob shrugged. 'I can tell 'em but I ain't their boss man. They ain't going to do nothink for me if the boss man don't say so.'

'Very well. We shall go as friends — unarmed,' the doctor said.

Morgan stared at the doctor in disbelief. 'But without muskets, sir, we could be dead as that sheep, look you.'

'Guns is for killing, ain't they?' the boy said scathingly. 'Think the blacks don't know that? 'Tain't no use telling 'em ye means no harm to 'em if ye got guns. They ain't glocky like youse lot.'

'Sound reasoning, Morgan,' the doctor agreed. 'One doesn't go armed when visiting friends. If we expect them to trust us we must first show that we trust them.'

'But I don't trust 'em, sir, and that's the long and short of it,' Morgan declared flatly.

Middleton placed a hand on his shoulder. 'Nevertheless, we go unarmed.'

An hour later the three were hidden in the scrub on the edge of the native campsite just beyond the flickering light of the ring of small camp fires. A circle of naked men, their limbs and bodies liberally daubed with white clay, loped slowly around in a circle, casting fantastic, ghostly shadows across the dusty arena. In the centre of the circle a single tall warrior, painted in bright symmetrical designs of red and yellow, stamped and swirled giddily, making the rainbow coloured parrot feathers around his head and neck dance as though with a life of their own. With the long hunting spear in his right hand he made sharp, threatening stabs at the smoky air. A wailing chorus from somewhere in the shadows was joined by the rhythmical clacking of small sticks struck together in perfect unison.

Rob regarded the scene with detached and amused interest: he had seen such performances before. Middleton squeezed his arm gently. 'What do you make of it, Rob? What's it all about?' he whispered.

The boy smiled knowingly. The meaning was quite plain to him. 'Them all painted white there, see? They'm sheep,' he explained softly. 'The big fella in the middle, he's their fight leader, Murringoo. He's showing 'em how he speared that sheep of yourn. Them others that's painted yella, they're your mob. You look...'

The painted dancers' prancing became faster and more furious as the tempo of the accompanying chorus quickened. At last, when it seemed that human feet could fly no faster and the dust rose in clouds that drifted away slowly into the outer darkness, the climax came suddenly. The long spear flashed through the air and its sharp point buried itself in the ground between the feet of one of the sheep. The white body fell to the ground in a writhing heap while the yellow dancers scuttled away in mock alarm, followed by the delighted laughter of the unseen audience. Rob chuckled quiet appreciation.

As the dust settled it became possible to observe the campsite clearly for the first time. Rob pulled at Middleton's jacket and pointed. The doctor looked across the open space to where a white man sat between two Aboriginal elders with long white beards and shaggy brows which shaded deep-set eyes glittering in the fire light.

'Reilly!' the doctor muttered, glancing at Morgan. The Welshman nodded.

'What do you suppose would happen, Rob, if I were to walk out there now, unarmed?' Middleton asked in a whisper.

'Most like, ye'd get a spear in ye,' the boy replied without hesitation.

'And what if you were with me?'

Rob considered the question. 'If youse was with me, I reckon they'd wait to see what we was going to do.'

Middleton stood up. 'Come along then. It's a good chance to face Reilly and have it out with him before these people. Heaven knows what he's been telling them about us.'

Morgan made as if to go with them but the doctor waved him back.'You stay hidden here and keep watch,' he ordered. 'If things don't go well for us you must do what you think best.'

The Welshman watched them anxiously as they slipped away together. Rob, with nothing to fear from his black friends, strode boldly into the firelight ahead of the doctor. The cheerful greeting he received was suddenly silenced by the sight of a white man behind him.

Morgan held his breath as Middleton followed Rob into the centre of the open, lighted place. He saw Reilly slowly rise to his feet, staring incredulously.

'What in the name of all the holy saints d'ye think to be doing here?' he heard him challenge the doctor.

The squatter had been caught off-guard but recovered quickly as he realised the security of his own position with the Aborigines. Suddenly he saw the unexpected meeting as a chance to damage the settlers once and for all in the eyes of the natives.

Middleton stopped in front of him, apparently unaware of any danger and greeted him like an old friend. 'Good morning, Mr Reilly,' he said, smiling. 'I'd not expected to meet you in the company of these good people.'

The man's scowl deepened. 'Did ye not hear me ask ye a question?' he demanded.

'I was about to ask you the same question, though in rather less biblical terms,' the doctor replied affably.

'I got the right to be here, damn ye!' Reilly retorted angrily.

Middleton's coolness was getting under Reilly's skin. His eyes flicked from side to side as he took in the ring of interested Aborigines, each with his small bundle of spears. He felt he was safe enough. 'Ye see?' he went on with a nod towards the men at his side. 'I'm one of 'em meself, in a manner of speaking.'

'I know,' Middleton responded. 'You have a wife and children among them, do you not?'

The man's eyes blazed. 'And what concern might that be of yours? It's a good Roman Catholic I am yet. Do ye believe I'd be after hitching meself to one of them wild heathens, do ye?' He thumbed contemptuously over his shoulder at a group of women who cowered into the shadows at his gesture.

'What I believe, Mr Reilly,' the doctor answered evenly, 'is that your black friends might not think so well of you if they knew you had been taking advantage of their kindness and generosity.'

Reilly turned and yelled at one of the women who approached him cautiously. She carried a small child who clung to her neck like a baby possum. The child's lighter colouring was obvious.

'Tell 'em agin what I been saying!' Reilly barked at her. 'Tell 'em agin in yer own lingo like you done already, d'ye hear me?' The woman nodded timidly. 'Tell 'em this is one of the white devils come to drive away all the animals and cut down the trees and burn all the grass and drive away all the black people! Tell 'em now's their chance to kill this 'un so's the rest of 'em will go away back where they come from. Go on! Tell 'em!'

Without taking her eyes from Reilly's face, the woman began to deliver a long shrill speech at the top of her voice. Middleton watched closely, trying to gauge the reaction of the tribesmen. He noticed uneasily that all the men were armed with half a dozen spears apiece and that when the woman's voice ceased there was an ominous stirring and murmuring among them.

Reilly looked around him, fiercely triumphant. 'Kill 'em! Kill the boy, too!' he raged, pointing at the doctor with one hand and making vicious stabbing gestures with the other.

The murmur of voices had died away and with the dark eyes of the warriors upon him, Middleton felt for the first time the cold shadow of fear.

Suddenly another shrill voice rang out from close beside him. 'Hark to me, all of youse!' Rob pointed at the doctor. He shouted. 'Him goodfella — gubba gubba! Him doctor.' The boy looked around him challengingly as he paused for breath then suddenly swung to face the squatter. He cried out to them pointing accusingly at Reilly.

All eyes were on Reilly now. He looked around for his woman to interpret for him but she had slipped away. He turned furiously on Rob. 'Now what in the devil's name might all that gab be about?'

Rob looked the Irishman straight in the eyes. 'I told 'em ye was a liar, Reilly. I told 'em as *he* was the goodfella and *youse* was a bad bastard as lies to 'em, see?'

Reilly rushed at the boy but Rob dodged smoothly and the half-crazed man found himself facing the doctor.

'Don't lay a hand on that lad!' Middleton warned him. 'He told the truth but your quarrel is with me, not with him.'

The two men glared at one another in silence, their fascinated black audience forgotten. At last Reilly spoke. 'So it's yerself I'll be after killing instead then. Take a spear in yer hand if ye're a man at all and let's have it out before these black heathens, the way they'll not forget it.'

He strode boldly up to the nearest native and snatched two spears at random from the bundle in his hand. He passed one of the spears to his opponent. 'Come on then. Are ye ready?'

Middleton made no attempt to take the spear. 'I didn't come here to fight,' he said quietly. 'We came in peace — unarmed.'

'Did ye now?' was the derisive reply. 'Then ye'd best change yer mind.'

'I don't believe you could kill in cold blood, Reilly, but if you did you'd be on the run for the rest of your life with the hangman close on your heels wherever you tried to hide.'

The man gave a scornful snort. 'There's good land across the mountains where a man could be safe and snug to the end of time. I seen it with me own two eyes, so I did.'

'Then what are we arguing about? Take your sheep and apply for a government grant. You're a free man and I'll support your application.'

'Is it soft in the head ye think me now? Fifty bloody acres they'd give me in all this great wilderness of land! And how many acres did you say they give to you and the leary bludger that come with ye?'

'We were allotted what we were entitled to under the law of the land. No more and no less.'

'Ah! So it's the law now, is it? Well, if it's the law ye're leaning on 'tis a weak thing indeed in these parts, mister. I wouldn't rely on it overmuch, if I was you.' The spear Middleton had ignored was now lying on the ground between them. The

102

squatter gave the end a kick and it slid through the dust, coming to rest at the doctor's feet. Still he made no move to pick it up. The blacks watched, motionless and silent, their dark eyes glowing. Slowly Reilly raised his spear and drew back his arm. 'Where will ye have it?' he asked through clenched teeth. 'It's all one to me.' The muscles in his right arm tightened as he prepared to launch the spear.

A sudden crashing in the scrub on the edge of the clearing caused every head to turn. The natives scattered, allowing Morgan's massive frame to come charging into the firelight like an infuriated bull and make straight for Reilly. The startled Irishman hurled his spear at his attacker but missed by a yard. He had no time to run before the blacksmith was upon him. Leaping high into the air, Morgan raised one great ham of a fist and brought it down like a pile driver on Reilly's skull. The man's knees buckled and he fell forward onto his hands, stars spinning wildly behind his drooping eyelids.

The Welsh giant stood over him like an angry colossus. 'If it's a fight you're looking for, boyo, I'm your man!' he roared.

Shaking his head to clear his blurred vision, Reilly staggered to his feet, backing away as he did so and sliding one hand inside his baggy shirt.

'Watch him, Morgan!' the doctor shouted. 'He has a pistol!'

Morgan's foot shot out, Reilly uttered a yell of pain and the pistol flew from his hand, discharging with a brilliant yellow flash and a bang which echoed eerily from side to side of the valley in the pre-dawn stillness.

The Aborigines pressed back still further and watched the astonishing spectacle provided by the white men. The squatter was now backing away, nursing his pistol hand injured by Morgan's heavy boot. Relentlessly Morgan followed him and, picking up the spear the doctor had ignored, began to rain furious blows on the man's head and shoulders. Reilly stumbled backwards, frantically trying to dodge the flailing shaft, then turned tail and scuttled into the dark haven of the bush.

At first the ensuing silence was broken only by Morgan's heavy breathing. Then Rob began to laugh as he recalled the cyclonic demolition of the enemy. The friendly blacks now crowded around him, gesticulating and dancing excitedly. Morgan regarded the gleeful group with bewilderment. He had expected an angry response from the natives, certainly to be attacked, perhaps to be speared but instead he heard only laughter and gleeful, excited chattering.

Middleton walked over to him, smiling. 'Thank you, Morgan. You did well to appear when you did. I'd not have let him spear me if I could have avoided it, you understand, but I was greatly obliged to you when you took matters out of my hands.' He clapped his companion on the back. 'And if they make good use of your performance at their next c'rrob'ree, it should be a theatrical event worth attending!'

Chapter 17

The Apprentice

Three months passed quickly and already changes were taking place in the valley. The Weatherbys now lived in a temporary homestead with thick, timber slab walls and the supreme luxury of rough, wooden flooring. Tents and huts for the assigned men had sprung up like mushrooms around the homestead site. Only when they were all weather-proof had Dr Middleton taken his own men and moved on a few miles up river to start work on his own property.

Halfway between the two homesteads stood the neatest building of all. One room, with walls of clean cut turf a foot thick, it stood on a sunny ten acre piece of flat land overlooking the river but safely above flood level. Its whitewashed walls were protected from sun and rain by a long, over-hanging roof of flattened bark. Some thirty yards away a smaller building served as a stable, the skillion roof of which had been extended to form an open lean-to, covering a forge, an anvil and the many other tools of the blacksmith's trade. All this was Morgan's property, a gift from Dr Middleton. Here he lived and worked, and with him, Rob. This unlikely alliance had come about after the fight with

Reilly in the Aboriginal camp. When one morning Rob had been describing the night's events to Thomas, he had been rudely interrupted by Prudence. 'I don't believe a word of it!' she had declared. 'He's making it all up.'

'Why should he make up such a story?' Thomas protested, deeply interested in Rob's description of the fight.

'Because he's a frightful little liar, that's why,' the girl retorted.

'Well, Morgan's just over there. Why don't you ask him?' Thomas challenged her.

'I will.' Prudence stalked over to the blacksmith who was replacing a broken axe handle. The boys followed her and Morgan looked up from his work as they approached. 'What happened at the Indians' camp the other night?' she demanded. 'Was there a fight?' She pointed at Rob. 'And was *he* there?'

'Was Rob there?' the Welshman repeated with a laugh. 'Indeed to goodness, yes! He saved Dr Middleton's life, I shouldn't wonder. A proper hero he was, I tell you. Ask the doctor if you don't believe me.' Prudence turned away, her cheeks colouring.

'And Rob said you gave that squatter fellow a good beating,' Thomas added eagerly.

'Oh, as to that,' Morgan replied modestly. 'I did give him a hard time, come to think of it. But no more than he deserved, look you.'

Whatever it was that had finally overcome Rob's distrust of Morgan, he was now the man's champion and inseparable companion. Of Reilly there was no sign since the night of the encounter. It was assumed that he had moved further up the valley, perhaps across the mountains to the remote,

106

limitless pastures he had boasted of discovering. No one ever reported sighting an Aborigine either, much to Dr Middleton's disappointment for he was still eager to make friends with them. 'They gone walkabout, that's all.' Rob had assured him. 'They'll come back agin, you see.'

Rob's dislike of hard work had been partly overcome by his admiration for Morgan's skill in the smithy. The roar of the forge, the showers of stinging sparks and the scalding hiss of steam as the red hot steel was plunged into cold water had frightened him at first but his fascination with the results had overcome his fear. At first his assistance had been limited to pumping the forge bellows but, encouraged by Morgan, he had tried his hand with the hammer and had even roughly formed a horse shoe all by himself. The thrill of making something with his hands and tools was new to him. The boy's attitude to other forms of labour was less enthusiastic. Digging he hated, especially the long trenches which Morgan seemed intent on creating. He grasped at every excuse for stopping, even to watch a mob of noisy kookaburras as they settled in a nearby tree and broke into their mocking, cackling chorus.

'Them bloody birds is laughing at us,' he remarked resentfully one spring day as he and Morgan worked together on the rich flat land behind the smithy. He leaned on the long handle of his shovel and gazed balefully into the tree.

Morgan glanced up happily without breaking the regular rhythm of his mattock stroke. 'Let them laugh,' he said. 'They've never seen men doing work like this before now, look you.'

'Me, neither,' Rob responded sourly. He tipped his homemade cabbage tree hat to the back of his head and wiped the sweat from his brow with a sun-tanned forearm. 'What the hell we digging this bloody trench for, Morgan?' he asked with sudden impatience.

Morgan's mattock stopped in mid-swing. He straightened himself then sat down on the side of the trench. He appeared to be thinking. 'Sit down, boyo,' he said at last, patting the turf beside him. 'I'll tell you why we're digging this trench.' Rob sat down beside him, glad of the rest. 'We're digging it because a gentleman named Mr Busby says so, that's why.'

'If there's good sense in it, I'll do it for youse but who's this old Busby cove?'

'Mr Busby? Farming superintendent, he was, at the Boys' Orphan School at Parramatta when I was working there waiting for my ticket-of-leave.' He looked at Rob shrewdly. 'I wonder they didn't send you there, you being a boy and an orphan and sorely in need of care and schooling.'

'They did,' Rob said. 'Two, three times but I bolted and they give up on me. They had me shovelling animal muck all day,' he went on indignantly. 'Then of a Sunday they made ye wash and listen to some glocky old geezer magging away in a church about summat.'

The blacksmith suppressed a smile with difficulty. 'It was all meant for your good, boyo, and if you'd stayed there you'd have met Mr Busby and you'd know why we're digging like this. He's writ a whole book about it.'

'About digging holes?' the boy asked incredulously.

'About growing grapes and making wine.'

Rob thought for a moment. 'What's grapes, then?'

'Grapes?' Morgan repeated, looking at him in surprise. 'You never seen grapes, boyo? Well, no, I suppose you wouldn't, the life you've been living. Grapes is like little plums. Sweet as sugar, grapes are', Morgan continued with enthusiasm. 'But they don't grow on trees, like plums; they grow on long stalks that come from little old dry sticks.'

The boy's eyes turned to a row of small, leafless twigs standing in a well-tended bed beside the cottage. 'Them things? How d'ye know them old sticks'll grow?'

'Because it's all writ down in Mr Busby's book,' Morgan explained, smiling confidently.

To his surprise, the boy's sceptical frown deepened. 'You can read?' he asked suspiciously.

'There's one you are for doubting! What use would a book be to me if I couldn't read it?'

'Ye're a liar!' Rob declared, glaring at him cynically.

The two stared at one another in silence. Then Morgan stood up, his face expressionless, and strode to the door of the cottage. He reappeared with a book held between his two great hands. Resuming his seat on the edge of the trench, he opened it carefully at the ornate title page. Pointing to each word with a thick, calloused finger, he began to read slowly. *A Tre-a-tise on the Culture of the Vine and the Art of Making Wine*. He turned to the boy questioningly and was about to continue when Rob spoke.

'Who learned ye?'

Honour satisfied, Morgan closed the book. 'My old mam it was taught me, bless her, with the Holy Bible on her knees.'

The resentment in the boy's manner softened as he looked at Morgan. 'Learning to read,' he said, 'That's real hard, ain't it? Only swells as can read proper.'

The blacksmith's face lit up. 'A swell, I am, is it?' He threw back his head and laughed then became suddenly serious. 'I'll make a bargain with you, boyo. You promise you'll stay here with me and not run away... and wash yourself in the river every day, same as me... and learn to keep a hold on that sharp tongue of yours... and I'll have you reading out of Mr Busby's book in no time.'

The boy gave a twisted smile at his companion's confidence but looked unconvinced.

'When you read this book', Morgan went on, tapping the cover with two fingers, 'you and me'll have it all inside here.' He tapped the side of his head with the two same fingers as if conveying the contents of the book into his brain. 'Mr Busby told me a man could make a handsome living from grapes and I've got ten acres here all made over, legal and proper, in Dr Middleton's own hand to Morgan Jones, Esquire. Esquire! That's me, look you!' He gazed slowly all around him at the fresh spring grass dotted with trees. 'I never thought to see the day,' he went on in a tone of awed wonder, 'when Morgan Jones would be called "Esquire" and live in his own cottage with his own smithy on his own ten acres. Yet here I am, a free man making a fresh start and me never so contented before in all my born days, I tell you!'

Rob was leaning back on his elbows, regarding Morgan through half closed eyes. It was the longest speech he'd ever heard him make.

'What's that other stuff then?' Rob asked.

'What other stuff?'

'That stuff you said — wine?'

Morgan looked shocked. 'Indeed to goodness, boyo, you must know what wine is?' His forehead wrinkled in thought. 'Wine is... wine is for drinking.'

'Can ye get lushed on it, same as rum?' Rob enquired shrewdly.

Morgan appeared pained by the question. 'If a man is fool enough to drink too much it'll make him tipsy as rum, I shouldn't wonder.'

Rob nodded approvingly. 'Then ye'll be able to sell it in Sydney town and make yer fortune. Them old lags'll soak it up.'

'You don't understand, boyo. Wine is not for convicts, look you; it's for gentlemen.'

'There ain't too many of them about,' the boy sniffed derisively. 'I wouldn't knock meself out digging no bloody trenches so a few swells can get lushed!'

Before Morgan could launch into a fuller description of wine, he was distracted by the sound of hooves in the distance. Both jumped to their feet and stared eagerly along the track that led to the Weatherby's homestead.

'It's them two kids,' Rob said, disappointed. 'In the buggy by 'emselves. Miss ain't with 'em.'

'There's strange it is,' Morgan said, equally

111

disappointed. 'I never knew them to come alone before.'

'If Miss was took sick,' Rob announced firmly, 'I'd go back to her and leave you, no matter what I said.'

The blacksmith's heart warmed to him. 'Better than any medicine, you'd be,' he replied. 'It's fond she is of you and no mistake.'

'What's that mean?' Rob asked suspiciously.

'Fond? That's when someone loves you, so there's lucky you are, indeed, boyo!'

'What's this 'ere "love" then?'

Morgan looked hard at him. 'This more of your gammon, eh?'

'No gammon!' Rob responded indignantly.

Morgan's eyes wandered to the pale blue sky. At least grapes and wine were things you could see and touch but love ...? 'It's a good warm feeling, is love,' he began uncertainly. 'It's a feeling I have for my old mam; a feeling she had for me. Your mam had it for you when you were a little babby.'

Rob considered this. 'Like I got for Miss then, eh?'

'I shouldn't wonder,' Morgan replied a little grudgingly.

'And like you got for her, eh?'

Morgan nodded. Words were beyond him.

'Youse and me, too, then,' Rob said in a tone of great satisfaction. 'She'd be a real good lackin, Miss,' he went on with a knowing air. 'She ain't no flash dollymop, Miss ain't.'

It was Morgan's turn to question the meaning of a word. 'She'd be a real good *what*?' he asked sharply.

'You heard,' Rob replied. 'A lackin is a skirt ye take to the church so the cove with the white choker round his neck can say them words out of a black book and then ye can shack up with her legitimate, see?'

'You mean... you mean...' Morgan stammered. 'You mean for me to take Mistress McInnes to wife?' he gasped at last.

'What's wrong with that then?' Rob demanded. 'Ain't she good enough for ye now?'

'Not good enough for *me*,? It's me not good enough for *her*, look you!'

The buggy rattled to a standstill beside them. Thomas secured the reins and jumped down. 'Hullo, Morgan! Hullo, Rob!' he greeted them brightly. 'I drove the buggy today all by myself.'

'Where's Miss?' Rob demanded abruptly. 'Why ain't she with ye?'

'If you mean McInnes,' Prudence retorted icily, 'she has her work to attend to. Mama said *we* might be entrusted with the buggy today.'

'We've brought you some blacksmith's work, Morgan,' Thomas said. 'There's an axle to be mended and some picks to be sharpened.'

'I'm much obliged to you,' Morgan replied as he lifted the broken axle and the pick heads from the buggy. 'Rob here will be glad of this work, too, for he doesn't take kindly to the mattock and shovel, I can tell you.'

Thomas had walked over to the trench and was looking into it curiously. 'Why are you digging such a long grave, Morgan?' he asked.

'A grave, is it?' Morgan gave a shout of laughter. 'Did you hear that now, Rob? A grave Master Thomas thinks it is. You tell him, boyo.'

Rob regarded Thomas coldly. 'Youse don't know nothink,' he remarked scornfully. 'Morgan and me's going to grow grapes in that there trench, see?'

'Grapes?' Thomas echoed in surprise. 'Wouldn't it be better to grow wheat or barley? You can't very well live on grapes.'

'Ye makes wine out of grapes,' Rob informed him with a patronising air. 'Wine is what the swells drink. Like rum, only better.'

'We know perfectly well what wine is,' Prudence stated from her lofty seat in the buggy, 'but I should be very surprised if you know anything about it.'

Rob grinned up at the girl cockily. 'He's got a book, see, Morgan has. It tells ye how to grow grapes and make wine out of 'em.' He turned to Morgan. 'Ain't that so now?'

Morgan nodded uncomfortably. He had no wish to pursue the discussion.

'And if he did have such a book,' the girl scoffed, 'who would read it to him?'

'He can read it hisself,' Rob announced triumphantly.

'I don't believe you!'

'Show her, Morgan! Show her!' Rob cried. The blacksmith drew the book from inside his shirt and held it up reluctantly. He was about to put it away again, hoping the subject was now over and done with when Prudence spoke again.

'What is the name of the book?' she asked with a superior smile.

Her disdainful air ruffled even the placid Morgan. He opened the book and read, slowly and carefully. *'A Treatise on the Culture of the Vine and the Art of Making Wine.'*

He looked up to make sure Prudence was paying attention. Her obvious astonishment gave him a warm feeling of satisfaction as he continued, ' "Compiled from the Works of Chaptal and Other French Writers and from the Notes of the Compiler during his Residence in Some of the Wine Provinces of France. By James Busby, Esquire". ' He closed the book gently and replaced it inside his shirt. Rob was grinning from ear to ear as he stared up at Prudence.

'Well?' he demanded. 'What ye got to say to that then, eh?'

The girl looked away, her face flushing. Thomas climbed back into the buggy and took up the reins. He gave Morgan and Rob a friendly smile which was his way of apologising for his sister's rudeness.

'Papa would like you to come over and fit the axle when you've repaired it,' he called.

'Tomorrow then, I shouldn't wonder,' the blacksmith answered with a cheerful wave.

As the buggy bumped away down the track, Morgan turned, eyes sparkling and a broad grin on his ruddy, bearded face. 'Come, Rob!' he cried with boyish excitement as he gathered up the heavy axle and made for the smithy. 'Bring in those pick heads and light up the forge. We'll have these few jobs done before dark if we work hard and tomorrow, first thing, we'll harness Betsy up to the sledge and pay a call on Mistress McInnes. Now there's happy you should be, boyo!'

115

Rob staggered into the smithy and dumped his heavy load on to the hard earth with a clatter.

'And tomorrow,' he said, pulling on a leather apron that hung from a peg in the wall, 'you'll tell Miss.'

Morgan lowered the axle on to the black charcoal of the forge and stared at the boy in alarm.

'Tell Miss? Tell her what?' he forced himself to ask.

'Don't ye mind what we was magging about when them two come?' Rob asked in surprise. 'Ye're going to tell Miss as we wants her to leave them swells and come and dab it up here with us.'

Morgan swallowed hard. 'Ah, now as to that, boyo,' he began, terrified at the thought of such a direct approach, 'there are matters beyond your understanding, you being just a lad...'

The boy's steady stare brought him to a faltering stop.

'If youse ain't game to tell her,' he said as he set a handful of kindling on the forge, 'then I will, see?'

Chapter 18

The Attack

The heavy axle took longer to repair than Morgan, in his eagerness to see Mandy again, had estimated and the forge continued to glow like a beacon in the wilderness long after dark. Rob's patience was beginning to wear thin. To his inexperienced eyes, smarting from the glare and heat of the fire, the axle had appeared straight and sound an hour ago. But Morgan was not satisfied. 'Just one more time, boyo,' he said encouragingly as they again swung the heavy bar from the anvil to the forge. He piled fresh charcoal on the growling crater of orange flame as Rob pumped the long wooden handle of the bellows.

Morgan straightened his back. He was naked from the waist up except for the thick leather apron that protected his chest from the flying sparks. He dabbed his face with a cloth and took a long drink of water from a blackened billy as he watched Rob's slim form moving wearily up and down with the arm of the bellows pump. 'Let me do that now, boyo.' He took the bar into his own tireless hands. 'Go you to the cottage and brew up a pot of tea for the both of us. I'll call if I need you. Off you go, now.'

The fire roared with renewed life as Rob slipped thankfully away. He had almost reached the cottage door when he froze, listening. From the smithy came the steady murmur of the forge but it was a sharper sound that had caught his ear. He backed away, silent as a shadow, into the shelter of a windbreak of trees near the cottage and pressed himself against the rough trunk of an ancient ironbark. From the dark depths of the trees came the subdued but unmistakable rustle of stealthily moving men — white men, his training with his Aboriginal friends told him.

To his ears their movements were clumsy and predictable; they were behind him, a little to his left and coming closer. Rob shrank into a dark hollow at the base of the tree and held his breath.

In the bright glow of the forge, Morgan stopped pumping and reached for a giant pair of tongs. He grasped the end of the white hot axle and dragged it on to the anvil. Picking up a ten pound hammer, he raised it above his head and was about to bring it down on the glowing metal when a voice stopped him.

'Ye can knock off work now, mister!'

Morgan turned swiftly, hammer poised, to look into the barrel of a musket held by a shadowy figure just outside the smithy. 'Who are you?' he asked, lowering the hammer slowly to his side.

The gunman took a couple of leisurely steps into the light from the forge, his sneering grin revealing broken, tobacco stained teeth. 'Reilly's the name,' he said. 'It's a poor memory ye have, surely.'

The bunched muscles in the blacksmith's shoulders relaxed. 'It's another beating you've come for then, is it?'

'Hold yer tongue, damn ye! Ye'll not lay a hand on me this time. I've a dozen others with me and not a black man among 'em!'

Morgan tossed the big hammer on to the forge and wiped the palms of his hands down the front of his apron. 'Now there's a simple liar you are, man,' he remarked coolly. 'You know as well as I do there aren't a dozen white men hereabouts could be out with you at this time of night. They're all assigned men who have to be accounted for after dark, isn't it?'

The man sneered. 'Did ye hear that, lads?' he called over his shoulder.

To Morgan's astonishment a chorus of gruff voices answered from the darkness. He looked at Reilly steadily, disguising his dismay. 'And what men may these be?' he asked

'Well now, 'tis a sad story, surely,' the Irishman answered readily. 'They was slaving away for Major Murdoch down the valley but I offered 'em work more to their liking and they come and joined me, so they did.'

'Then if you're telling the truth, the major will see you hang for it.'

Reilly laughed. 'That's where ye're wrong entirely — eh, lads?'

Again the invisible chorus. The man's eyes narrowed. 'The major's hanging days are over for it's himself we took the liberty of hanging first!'

Morgan's heart sank but he showed no sign of alarm. 'There's foolish you were then,' he commented, apparently unmoved. 'You'll dance on the end of a hangman's rope though the major won't be there to enjoy it.'

He untied the strap of his apron and slipped it over his head with the unhurried air of a man finishing work. 'A dozen of the major's men you have, is it? What of the rest of them?'

'It was a free choice I give 'em — to come with me or go their own ways. It's yourself has the same choice, blacksmith. I bear ye no grudge. Ye're not an old lag like us but you come out under a hatch jest the same.'

Reilly paused. His manner had lost some of its hostility. The musket barrel was lowered as Morgan's apparently calm acceptance of the situation took the edge off his vigilance. 'We could make good use of a smith such as yerself,' he went on. 'Join me and the lads and it's a free man ye'll be once again.'

Morgan regarded the man thoughtfully as though considering the proposal, the leather apron hanging idly from his hand. Suddenly the apron thrashed the air, wrapping itself around the barrel of the musket which discharged harmlessly into the ground. Before Reilly could recover from the surprise attack, Morgan had seized him, swung him around and held him firmly before him as a shield while he backed up against the smithy wall. The convicts rushed in, each with a musket from Major Murdoch's well-stocked armoury.

'Don't shoot! Don't shoot!' Reilly yelled, writhing in the giant Welshman's grasp. 'Take him with your hands!'

Four men lay unconscious by the time Morgan was overpowered. Gasping and bloody, his wrists and ankles bound, he was tied to the central hardwood post that supported the smithy roof. Reilly was all for finishing him off there and then but his companions, though battered and sore, outvoted him. Morgan was, after all, one of them and not of the hated 'aristocracy'. It would be enough, they argued, to leave him securely bound to the post where he had an even chance of being found before he died of thirst.

The rebels were in no hurry to depart after their recent exertions. Gloating over their success so far, they discussed their future plans as they boiled their billies on the forge and tucked into food from the cottage. Next they were going to raid Weatherby's place. After that it would be Middleton's turn and, when all the livestock was rounded up from the valley, they would cross the hills to the west and thence, by a route known only to Reilly, overland to the new settlements on the Hawkesbury River. There everything would be sold and the proceeds divided.

When the gang prepared to leave they made a final effort to persuade Morgan to join them but he had no illusions about the fate of anyone proved to have had any dealings with these men. One remote chance of help remained in Morgan's mind: what, he wondered, had become of Rob? He dared not ask in case Rob had not been discovered yet it seemed strange that there had been no mention of him.

The men left and Morgan heard Betsy being taken from the stable and the horses galloping off.

The thought of Reilly descending on the sleeping Weatherby homestead with his pack of ruffians, triumphant, vengeful and with nothing to lose since the hanging of Major Murdoch, roused him to furious effort. He inhaled deeply to expand his chest and flexed the powerful muscles of his arms and shoulders, trying to stretch and loosen the ropes. He twisted from side to side, his fingers groping for a knot. He felt the post move slightly and it came to him that if he could uproot it he might be able to release himself by sliding the ropes off the pole. He rocked his great frame violently and felt the post loosening. With rising hope he threw himself into the struggle, bringing sheets of bark raining down from the smithy roof. He paused, gathering strength for a second onslaught, when he heard a familiar voice behind him.

'What ye trying to do? Shake the bloody place down?'

'Rob!' Morgan gasped. 'They didn't catch you then?'

'Them?' the boy replied witheringly. 'I knowed they was coming miles off.'

Morgan heard the crisp sound of a sharp blade slicing through his bonds and felt them loosen and fall away. 'I thought they'd got you, boyo,' he said as he tore impatiently at the remaining ropes. 'I thought Reilly might have...'

'I ain't glocky! I played possum on 'em like the blacks and they walked right past me.' He paused. 'What we going to do now, Morgan?'

As he rubbed the circulation back into his chafed and bruised limbs, Morgan told Rob what he had heard. Concerned only for Mandy's safety, the boy was all for racing after the gang and he struggled angrily when Morgan held him back.

'It's no use going after them, Rob,' Morgan told him. 'We can't get to the Weatherby's place before them, look you, so we can't stop them. Go you the other way, boyo, to Dr Middleton's and tell him. Run fast as you can so he'll be ready for them. That's the only way we'll catch them! You want to catch them, don't you?'

The boy gave a surly nod. Morgan was right, he knew, but it was hard to force his feet in one direction when his heart wanted to be off in another. The blacksmith watched him vanish into the darkness then set off himself to give what help he could to the Weatherby's. Reilly's men had not long left when Morgan arrived and the dozen or so men who had refused to join the gang were mostly older convicts nearing the ends of their sentences. They were gathered in a bemused, frightened group, watching helplessly as flames lit up the windows of the homestead building. Morgan quickly took charge and organised a bucket chain from the well.

Mr Weatherby had been knocked out and left for dead. His wife had fainted and when Morgan found them they were both recovering slowly. Neither knew what had become of Mandy and the two children and it was from one of the assigned men that he learned all three had been taken away as hostages.

'My God!' Mr Weatherby exclaimed when he heard the news. 'We must go after them at once!'

That was impossible, Morgan explained, for all the horses, muskets, powder and shot had been taken so that pursuit was out of the question. Their only hope was that Rob would reach Dr Middleton in time to warn him of the coming attack.

Rob had reached the Middleton homestead in record time. The doctor took the news with the calmness of a naval man trained to deal with sudden emergencies. He aroused Jake Brightwell. 'Can you use a musket, Jake?' he asked the surprised convict. 'Because if you can, now is your chance to repay any debt you may fancy you owe me.' Jake's eyes gleamed in the lamplight as the emergency was explained to him. 'All I have are three double-barrelled muskets and a pair of sporting pistols, all with percussion caps, not flintlocks', the doctor said. 'I'll show you how to use them.' He turned to Rob. 'How about you, lad? Do you know how to load a musket?'

'I reckon I will if ye show me.'

'Yes, I'm sure you will,' the doctor said with a quick smile at the boy's confidence. 'I'll soon teach you how to load and to prime with a cap.'

With Rob loading for them, the doctor hoped that he and Jake could give Reilly the impression that he was up against a much larger armed force and so hold off an attack but, not satisfied with simply holding the gang off, he discussed a further plan with Jake. 'What's your opinion of the loyalty of the other men, Jake? Can they be trusted, d'you think?'

The convict lovingly stroked the smooth butt of the gun in his hand. 'Mister,' he said with quiet sincerity, 'them men'd fight for you agin the king of England hisself if need be!'

'I'm hardly likely to put them to that test,' he said, 'but it did cross my mind that if the men were armed with pick handles and pitchforks and told to wait until we had drawn the enemy's fire, they might lay about them to good effect without much risk to themselves before Reilly's men have time to reload. What do you say to that, Jake?'

Jake smiled broadly. 'I tell you straight, mister, they'd take real kindly to the chance of splitting a few heads, legal like.'

'Tell them,' Middleton called after Jake as he left to wake the other men, 'there will be a special issue of rum after it's all over.' Picking up one of his double-barrelled muskets, he turned to Rob. 'Watch me carefully,' he said. 'Loading is quite simple but you must be sure about one thing, Rob. Never be tempted to ram too much lead into the barrel of a musket...'

'Why not?' the boy interrupted. 'The more the better, ain't it?'

The doctor looked at him sternly. 'You do exactly as I show you, Rob. One ball and one ball only. Too much and it'll burst the breach of the gun open and most likely kill the man firing it. Remember that!'

The eastern horizon was beginning to glow with a soft orange light when Rob, apparently asleep on the floor, suddenly sat up. Jake and the doctor, each seated at an open window with a loaded musket across his knees, looked around. 'They're coming,' the boy said.

Jake frowned. 'How can ye tell?'

Rob got to his feet and crossed to the window beside the convict. He stood listening for a few moments, head on one side, then turned to Jake pityingly. 'Ye must be deaf then. Can't ye hear 'em? Five... six horses coming from the other side of the hill.'

'Only five or six, Rob?' Middleton asked anxiously. 'Are you quite sure?'

'Course I'm sure! It'll be light enough to see 'em when they come over the hill.'

The two men stared in the direction of the hill. In the distance a kookaburra's strident laughter announced the new day and against the empty silence it left behind they could just make out the steady drumming of hooves. A few moments later five horsemen cantered over the hill and reined in before the homestead. One rider raised an arm, an orange flame stabbed the sky and the sharp report of a pistol echoed through the still, dawn air. The five horsemen spread out and waited for a response. 'Who's there?' Middleton called.

'No friend of yourn, mister!' came the Irishman's prompt reply. 'Come out with yer hands over yer head if ye've a mind to save yer life.' He waited impatiently for an answer, puzzled and angered by the silence.

'D'ye hear me, mister?' he shouted. 'We're clearing out the valley of all youse illegitimates and it's only yourself is in danger. All your men are free to join with us or go their own ways, whichever they fancy.' Again he waited in vain for some response. 'Come on out, mister, with yer hands over yer head if you don't want us to start shooting...'

'That,' murmured the doctor, 'is precisely what we do want you to do.' He glanced at Jake, crouched at the window, cheek pressed against the butt of his musket. 'Perhaps you would like to open the proceedings, Jake?'

Jake squeezed the trigger. A spear of flame pierced the half light and the thunderous explosion made Rob's ears ring. The horses reared up, unseating one man who quickly clambered back into the saddle.

'That's the way of it, is it?' Reilly yelled. 'Let 'em have it, lads!'

Five musket shots rang out in quick succession and five lead balls flattened themselves against the hardwood slab wall of the homestead. Jake's gun belched flame and thunder as he pulled the second trigger of the double-barrelled musket. A howl of pain came from one of the men who dropped musket and reins and slid to the ground as his horse galloped off in panic.

'Good shooting, Jake!' Middleton exclaimed. 'That's one bird to you. Let's see if I can make it a brace.' He fired but the remaining four riders were fighting to keep their horses under control and the shot went wide. He let fly with his second barrel, making the horses buck and rear even more wildly.

Suddenly bedlam broke loose as the assigned men, eager to play their part, rushed from cover brandishing picks, shovels and pitchforks and yelling like banshees. It was too much for the horses; they turned and bolted in terror, unseating two more riders. The doctor thrust his musket into Rob's hands and ran outside. Three men lay on the ground surrounded by a shouting, laughing mob of excited convicts. One was dead with Jake's ball in his shoulder and his neck broken in falling from his horse, a second had been clubbed unconscious and the third was moaning with pain as he nursed a broken arm.

When the three had been carried inside, Middleton addressed the men. 'I promised you a ration of rum,' he said, 'and you shall have it just as soon as the sun rises. But I promise you something better than that: when I report this affair to the Governor in Sydney every man jack of you shall be mentioned by name.'

As the soft light of morning spread across the sky, Rob watched the doctor bandaging the broken arm. 'Is he hurt bad?' he asked, trying to appear unmoved by the man's flinching and groaning.

'Just a simple fracture,' Middleton replied. 'He's lucky to have got off so lightly.' He supported the man's arm in a sling then asked brusquely, 'What's your name?'

'Bolton, sir. Abraham Bolton,' the convict answered nervously.

'One of Major Murdoch's men, eh?'

'Aye, sir, but I had nowt to do with his hanging, that I swear to! I was dead set agin it, sir! Tried to stop 'em, I did, but they took no heed of me. They wouldn't let me stay behind like I wanted to on account of me knowing summat of horses and muskets, sir, and that's the God's truth, I swear to it!'

Middleton regarded the man cynically. 'My young friend here,' he said with a nod towards Rob, 'has a very useful word — "glocky". Is that what you think I am to believe such a story?'

'It's the God's truth I'm telling you, sir! Ask the womenfolk — they'll tell you. It was me as told 'em to run away and hide in the woods afore Reilly come up to 'em. They'll remember that, I warrant, sir.'

The doctor's expression softened a little. 'And what of the womenfolk? Are they safe? Tell me exactly what happened and if what you say about your part is true I'll put in a good word for you. So speak up, man.'

Eagerly the man described the raid on the Weatherby homestead. 'Reilly reckoned as all Mr Weatherby's men would come over to him but only three was willing,' he ended. 'So Reilly put a light to the house and took the two kids and the woman away with him.'

'What woman?' Rob demanded at once.

'You mean Mrs Weatherby?' Middleton suggested.

'No, I never caught sight of her, sir. It was the servant girl, the Scotch one. She was with the young 'uns trying to hide 'em when Reilly seen 'em. He reckoned it'd be a slow job getting away with all them animals so if anyone come after him, he'd have a hold over 'em with the woman and the kids, see?'

The doctor whistled softly and turned to judge Rob's reaction to the news but the boy was no longer with him. Through the open door he saw him disappearing into the dawn mist not, strangely, in the direction of the Weatherby's place but up river into the back lands. 'Rob!' he called. 'Where are you going? Come back!'

The boy ran on with the tireless, pounding gait of an emu. If he had heard, he gave no sign.

Chapter 19

A Traitor in the Camp

Reilly, shocked and not a little scared by his reception at Middleton's, had galloped back with his sole surviving companion to rejoin the other men, convinced that they must put as much distance as possible between themselves and the valley — and quickly. To Murdoch's livestock had now been added the animals stolen from the Weatherby property and slow progress had been the result during the day. Finally, as darkness fell, they had camped beside a stream at which the exhausted animals could be revived ready for another hard day's travelling.

The attack on the Weatherbys' homestead had taken place late in the evening. Prudence and Thomas had been in bed but Mandy had snatched up their clothes and shepherded them outside to dress hurriedly in the dark. When Reilly had discovered them and hit upon the idea of taking them as hostages, only Thomas was wearing boots so Mandy and Prudence had been set bareback on a horse which Thomas led with a bridle. Now, at the end of the first day's journey, the three were huddled together under a stringybark tree, weary, sore and frightened.

Some distance away around a fire, several men were making damper and brewing billies of tea. They were listless, tired and argumentative. Their confidence in their leader had received a setback after the loss of three of their companions and they were in a critical mood.

'He was lying in wait for us, I tell ye,' Reilly insisted irritably, trying to justify the morning's defeat.

'How the hell could he know we was coming?' a sceptical voice growled.

'It's yerself should ask him that!' Reilly snapped back. 'He's a Navy man, ain't he? He sleeps with a loaded gun by his side.'

'Sam reckons there were four shots,' a third voice put in.

'That's right,' Sam confirmed as he juggled with a boiling billy. 'There was more than just him, I'll take me 'davy on it. Besides, his men was all ready and waiting. As soon as we fired our pieces we had no time to reload afore they all come a-swarming out at us and yelling like devils and frightened the hell out of the horses.' Reilly grunted grudging agreement. 'That's how three of us got took,' Sam concluded, 'and it's them'll swing for what we done, that's the God's truth.'

'And they ain't the only ones as'll swing neither if we ain't bloody lucky,' a wiry little Cockney chimed in. 'We should of left the woman and them kids behind, Reilly. They'll never give up on us so long as we got them.'

Several of the others murmured uneasy agreement.

'It's the fool of the world y'are, Dodger,' Reilly blustered. He rounded on the man, eyes blazing. 'D'ye not see how it is?' He pointed at the little group under the stringybark tree. 'So long as we got them with us they dursn't come near us for fear of the hurt we can do to 'em. If they was your kids now, would you want to find 'em with their throats slit, now would ye?'

He nodded towards Mandy and the children. 'Take 'em some damper and a billy of tea,' he ordered. 'And God help any man as interferes with 'em unless I gives the word!'

After they had eaten, Mandy leaned back against the tree and gathered Prudence and Thomas to her, an arm around each and, in her warm, comforting embrace they both quickly fell asleep. It took Mandy herself some time to sleep, partly because she wanted to keep watch on the men and partly from the discomfort of her position which she could not change without disturbing the children. Finally, despite vigilance and cramped limbs, she dropped off into an uneasy doze.

Then, as in a dream, she heard a voice whispering close to her ear. Her eyes flew open. Prudence and Thomas were still fast asleep. She must have been dreaming, she decided. She stirred slightly to ease the numbness in her arms and legs.

'Don't move, Miss,' the whisper came again. 'Don't move. It's me — Rob.'

Now she was wide awake. 'Rob,' she breathed. 'Ye'd best not let them find ye for they're wicked, desperate men.'

'They ain't going to get me,' came the quiet, confident reply. 'They got two men watching the sheep and cows and horses and one at the fire and they're all snoring.'

The man at the fire suddenly woke with a grunt and gaped foolishly around the silent camp. Mandy's heart thumped and she held her breath as the man stood up and stared suspiciously in her direction. He turned away, seeing only the little group of three huddled at the base of the tree. Kicking some sticks into the glowing embers of the fire, he yawned and lowered himself wearily into his old seat. In a few minutes he was fast asleep again.

Mandy sensed a movement behind her but dared not turn to look. 'He never saw nothink,' she heard Rob whisper.

'What are ye going to do now?' she whispered in return.

'Going to sleep by the fire.'

'But they'll find ye there in the morning!'

'I ain't glocky, miss. Wait and see...'

Mandy watched anxiously as the boy slid noiselessly over the rough ground to within a few feet of the sleeping guard. There he found a shallow depression warmed by the fire and curled up like a cat to sleep.

The first rays of the sun were slanting through the trees when Mandy and the two children were rudely awakened by the bellowing voice of Reilly. 'How the hell did he get here?' the Irishman roared, pointing at Rob sitting cross-legged beside the fire gnawing at what looked like a fish which he held firmly in both hands.

The rest of the gang struggled to their feet, stumbled towards the fire and regarded the intruder with varying degrees of sleepy interest.

'It's only Maggie Jackson's kid,' one ventured, as though that explained everything.

'I know who it is!' Reilly bawled. 'How did the little sod get here is what I'm wanting to know.' He turned angrily on the man beside the fire. 'Was it not yerself was guarding the camp from the middle of the night?'

The man scratched his head as he looked at Rob. 'I never seen him come,' he replied simply. A second man approached the boy and stood over him. 'What's that ye're eating?' he demanded hungrily.

Rob spat out a small bone as he continued to chew. 'Sand lizard, roasted,' he said. 'Good scran! Want some?' He held up the half eaten reptile hospitably but the man recoiled, grimacing. 'Bloody little Injun,' he muttered.

'Never mind what he's eating!' Reilly barked. 'Tell me how he was getting here and us none the wiser.'

The boy stood up and his strong teeth tore a last piece of flesh from the lizard's carcass before he tossed the remains onto the fire where it remained, sizzling and spitting. Chewing with relish, he faced the Irishman. 'I got as much right here as youse, Reilly.'

'Ye young spalpeen...' Reilly began menacingly.

'Leave him be!' Dodger's cockney voice sang out. 'The kid won't do no harm and if we ever get lost he'll be as good as an Injun guide.' Several men supported this idea.

134

'We ain't going to get lost,' Reilly retorted. 'I been this way afore, did ye not hear me say so?' In spite of his apparent confidence, he hesitated and glowered at the boy 'He gulled me once afore, the young limb of Satan...'

Rob sensed the man's weakening. 'If I comes with ye, Reilly,' he said, 'ye'll have to give me a nag.'

'Like hell! Ye'd be off with it as soon as a man's back was turned!'

Rob shrugged as though it was of little interest to him. 'I ain't walking and that's flat.'

'If he's wanting to come with us we can easy spare a hoof for him,' Sam said.

'Ye had them two judies up on a nag yesterday,' the boy pointed out, looking across to Mandy and the Weatherby children who were watching and listening anxiously. 'Give me a hoof and ye can put the other kid up behind me. If ye keep him going on his feet, he'll squib out on ye.'

'He's fly, this one,' Dodger declared admiringly. 'Don't miss a thing, he don't. Give him a hoof, Reilly, like he says and he can keep jack on them three for us. He won't give no trouble. I'll go bail for him. He's family, ain't he?'

There was general agreement with Dodger's belief that Rob could be trusted. Reilly was not convinced. 'No saddle, though,' he stated with finality.

'I never asked for no saddle.'

Thomas was delighted when he found he was to ride bareback behind Rob but could not understand why his attempts at conversation were met with silence. After a while he gave up and the pair plodded along behind Mandy and Prudence, followed by a mob of sheep badly herded and, like the cattle, frequently breaking away and having to be rounded up with much shouting and cursing by the handful of men who could ride well enough. Their slow progress made sense of Reilly's taking hostages.

Late in the afternoon Rob spoke at last. 'Can ye hear me good?' he asked, looking straight ahead and keeping his voice low.

'Yes, I can hear you,' Thomas replied eagerly.

'Well, shut up and hark!'

They jogged along for some time before Rob spoke again, cautiously as before. 'If Reilly seen us magging he'd stop us riding together, see? He don't trust me but I reckon he's forgot that by now...' He broke off as one of the men cantered by to join the leaders. 'I told Miss when you two was asleep last night as no harm would come to ye'cos I was seeing to it.'

'You mean you're going to save us?' Thomas broke in, forgetting the order to listen and say nothing.

'Keep yer trap shut, can't ye?' Rob growled.

Thomas waited, bubbling inwardly with curiosity and hope.

'Ye done me a good turn in Sydney,' Rob went on at last, 'so I'm paying ye back for it. Trouble is, I got to trust ye.'

'Oh, you can trust me,' Thomas whispered earnestly.

'Ye won't gab? Not to Miss nor that glocky skirt of yourn, neither?'

'You mean Prudence? Oh, no! Certainly not if you say so. On my honour.'

136

'What the hell does that mean?'

'On my solemn word of honour as a gentleman,' Thomas whispered, 'I promise faithfully not to tell anyone what you say to me...'

'I dunno about all that gammon,' Rob said. 'And hold yer gab now.'

Half an hour passed in silence then Thomas felt Rob's elbow in his ribs. 'Tonight,' Rob said, 'when they're all asleep, I'm going to fix 'em.'

'How?'

'Never ye mind. Just do as I bid ye. I'm going to wake ye so ye can keep an eye on 'em for me. I'm going to fix'em one by one, see, and if one of 'em wakes up, ye got to jump up and start yelling like hell...'

'What for?' Thomas asked in a worried tone.

Rob swallowed his impatience. 'So they'll think it was youse woke him, not me, ye fool! Give me a chance to cover, see? If they catches me at it they'll cut me bloody froat — no gammon!' A long pause followed. 'All ye got to do if one of 'em wakes is start yelling and screaming fit to wake 'em all. Tell 'em ye was having a dream or summat. It don't matter what ye tell 'em so long as I got a chance to go to ground. They won't touch youse.' Another long pause. 'That's the lay, see? It's a fakement. Ye're the stall so I can knock over the job.'

Thomas's head buzzed with confusion but he dared not ask any more questions. It was clear that he was expected to keep watch while Rob did whatever he was planning to do and if any of the men should wake in the middle of it, it was his job to create a noisy diversion.

137

'Remember ye swore ye wouldn't sing!'

Sing? Thomas shook his head. He had no recollection of having promised anything of the sort but if Rob didn't want him to burst into song nothing would make him do it.

Chapter 20

Captain Devereau

After Rob left, Dr Middleton rounded up all his animals and men, loaded the two wounded convicts onto a wagon and set off to join his forces with what was left at the Weatherbys' place. They reached the smoking remains of the Weatherby homestead by mid-morning. The doctor attended to the injured then galloped off down the valley with Morgan and an extra horse to help the survivors at Murdoch's place. Having done what he could to help there, he sent Morgan back to take charge at Weatherby's and set off by himself on the long ride to the military outpost at Wallis Plains on the road to Newcastle. The night was well advanced by the time his two lathered horses clattered to a stop beside the barrack's hitching rail. A sergeant hurried to help him as he slipped wearily from the saddle and led him into the office of the garrison's commander.

'Lieutenant Williams will be with you directly, sir,' he said as Middleton lowered himself gratefully into a chair. It had been a long day and a long ride.

A young lieutenant entered the office hastily, pulling on his jacket. He was followed by a second, older, officer. The lieutenant dropped into a chair behind his desk. 'First Lieutenant Henry Williams,' he announced briskly, '40th Regiment of Horse, Officer Commanding this post.' He indicated the second officer who had taken up a position against the wall, a little way from the desk, as if not wishing to intrude. 'This is Captain Devereau of the Indian Army who happens to be here on furlough,' he explained. 'He is naturally concerned to know what has taken place and to do anything he can to help.'

'You must understand, sir, that I am merely a visitor, a guest of Lieutenant Williams,' the captain added, 'but if there is anything I can do...'

Middleton described the events of the previous day as Lieutenant Williams regarded him importantly. 'This is an extremely serious affair,' he commented. 'The first affair of its kind since I've been stationed here...'

'It is serious, indeed!' Captain Devereau agreed. He turned to the lieutenant. 'If Mr Williams is prepared to delegate his authority to me I would gladly take a company of men and run these villains down.'

'You're most welcome, Captain,' Williams replied readily. 'I have only twenty men and a sergeant as well as myself. You may take half of them and the sergeant, too. He's a very reliable fellow.'

'Then we shall leave at dawn,' the captain announced, turning to Middleton. 'That will give you time for a meal and a few hours sleep, sir.'

The little troop set off at first light, Devereau cantering alongside Middleton at the head of the column. 'This looks to be a most agreeable country,' the captain remarked. 'I broke my journey from

140

Calcutta because I was asked by an old friend in England to spy out some land for him in New South Wales and His Excellency, the Governor, recommended the valley of the Hunter River. So, you see, we should have met in a few days. Tell me frankly, sir, this present calamity aside, have you any regrets about coming here to settle?'

Middleton considered his reply carefully. 'You might search the world as I have done,' he said with quiet sincerity, 'and never come across more perfect virgin soil. The climate, too, is tolerable; neither too hot in summer nor too cold in winter. We even have a blacksmith with us who proposes to grow grapes and make wine.'

'A blacksmith, eh?' The captain was most impressed. 'A useful man to have away out here.'

'Indeed, yes! And I confidently predict that before a dozen years have passed there will be a vineyard and a prosperous village where his smithy now stands.'

'Then I take it you would recommend my friend to acquire land hereabouts?'

'Most certainly! What extent of land does your friend have in mind?'

'Oh,' came the airy reply, 'somewhere around thirty or forty thousand acres...'

'Good God!' Middleton exclaimed in astonishment. 'As much as that? Then it may not be so easy as you think. A grant of that size is beyond the Governor's power to make. It would have to be approved by the Secretary of State in Westminster — Lord Bathhurst.'

'There should be no difficulty there,' Devereau replied casually. 'My friend is closely acquainted with Lord Bathurst. I fancy there is even some remote family connection.'

'I see.' The doctor rode along in silence for a while. 'Would it be impertinent to ask the name of your friend? He would seem to be a person of some importance.'

The captain gave a rueful smile. 'I can tell you only in the strictest confidence. He already owns large estates in England and it might embarrass him if it ever became known he was considering the purchase of more land here. We were at school together, you see, and when we went up to Oxford my friend suffered a tragedy of a very private and personal nature. As a result, he decided that as soon as he was able he would leave England and start a new life elsewhere. I agreed to go with him. Then, only last year, a most unfortunate accident occurred by which my friend inherited titles and estates that keep him in England a great deal of the time.'

'Your friend's father met his death unexpectedly?'

'No, no! His two elder brothers were drowned at sea thus making him heir to the earldom of Yarville. The shock hastened his father's death and so the plans we had made for our future together were destroyed at a stroke.'

'Yet you are still here to find land for him?'

'He is a wealthy man now and has generously offered to provide the money if I can find suitable land. We shall still be partners and I will manage the property on his behalf.'

The doctor chuckled as a thought struck him. 'An earl in the valley, if only as an absent owner, would certainly make our Mrs Weatherby very happy!'

'Your Mrs Weatherby has a weakness for earls?' the captain enquired, smiling.

Middleton laughed. 'Mrs Weatherby is my neighbour and a quite outrageous snob. She is the daughter of a Lancashire mill owner and married the youngest son of a baronet. She is passionately devoted to the aristocracy of which she fancies herself a part.'

'You seem to have interesting neighbours in the valley,' the captain remarked.

'Interesting, indeed! Even Reilly, the squatter we are pursuing, once had my sympathy in some respects. Then there is Morgan Jones, our Welsh blacksmith and Mandy McInnes, a Scottish lass who does her best as Mrs Weatherby's maid. Poor Mandy! She has a lot to put up with! Then there is Rob, the lad who gave me warning of the attack. He's probably the most interesting character of all.'

'A most extraordinary youth from your account,' the captain agreed.

'That boy has probably saved my life twice over,' Middleton went on seriously, 'but it's difficult to know how best to repay him.'

As the two men rode along together, the doctor related as much of Rob's history as he knew.

'His mother's name was Maggie Jackson, you say?' Devereau asked at the end.

'That is so. But where the unfortunate woman came from or why she was transported is impossible to discover out here now that she is dead.'

They rode on in thoughtful silence.

143

Chapter 21

Conspirators

Anxious to keep well ahead of pursuit, Reilly pushed his men even harder on the second day so that it was a very weary party that finally settled down for the night. Thomas helped Mandy and his sister to make themselves as comfortable as possible, then announced that he would bed down a little apart from them, explaining that he thought they would all sleep more easily if they were not huddled together as on the previous night. Mandy readily agreed.

The camp was soon sound asleep. Even the two men keeping first watch quickly dropped off after a brief pretence of vigilance. Thomas remained awake to see what Rob would do but even he was overcome at last. He was awakened by a gentle shake and found Rob crouched beside him.

'Mind now,' Rob whispered. 'If any of 'em wakes, start yelling! If they gets me...' He drew a finger across his throat.

Thomas nodded. His own throat was suddenly dry and tight.

Rob slipped away and Thomas watched with bated breath as he approached the nearer of the two sleeping guards. He reminded Thomas of a lizard moving with infinite caution towards an unwary insect. His hand moved out slowly towards the man's musket lying on the ground beside him. The man stirred in his sleep, grunting as he made himself more comfortable against the tree trunk. Rob froze, hand poised over the gun. Thomas's heart thudded. It seemed an age before Rob's hand moved again and picked up the musket which disappeared with him into the shadows behind the tree. What happened there Thomas could not see but he scarcely breathed until a minute or two later the gun was carefully replaced and Rob faded like a ghost into the night.

Not all the men were visible from where Thomas lay propped up on an elbow, wide-eyed and staring, but wherever a man lay sleeping Rob was sure to appear, unhurried and silent, to carry out his mysterious mission. Thomas's nerves tingled. He was ready to leap up screaming at the slightest sign of trouble. His early worry, that he might let Rob down by falling asleep, now seemed absurd.

Suddenly Rob was at his side again. 'Ye can stop peeping now and get some kip,' he said under his breath. 'I knocked it over. No flummut.'

Thomas gasped with relief. 'You mean... you've done it?'

'That's what I said, didn't I?' He slipped noiselessly back to his place on the far side of the fire and curled up to sleep.

Reilly had the camp astir at dawn and, as the rising sun brought light and warmth to the valley, Thomas looked around warily for signs of Rob's work. Everything seemed to be exactly as it was the night before and, after a quick breakfast of dry damper and sweet tea, the company prepared to move on.

Rob led his horse to where Thomas was helping Mandy and Prudence to mount. 'Hey!' he called softly. 'Hold this 'un. I'll help 'em.'

Thomas took the reins from him and watched as Mandy settled herself on the horse's back and Rob pretended to make an adjustment to the bridle.

'Don't ye be feared, Miss,' he said, keeping his voice low. 'Today ye'll be free, cross me heart.'

Mandy gathered up the reins with a worried frown. 'But I'm afeared for ye, Rob...'

The boy gave her foot a friendly pat. 'Don't ye be feared for none of us, Miss. Today ye'll be free. Take me oath on it!'

A movement behind him made Thomas turn 'Look out, Rob!' he cried.

He was too late. Reilly had darted past him and confronted Rob, his expression an ugly mixture of hatred and triumph. The boy made a bolt for it but the Irishman stuck out a foot and Rob sprawled on the ground. Reilly bent down, grabbed him by the hair and hauled him to his feet.

'So it's their freedom you're about to give 'em this day, is it?' he snarled. Still holding him by the hair, he struck Rob viciously across the face. The blow made Rob's head spin but he uttered no sound as he stared back at the man defiantly.

Mandy slid from the horse's back. 'Leave him be!' she stormed.

Reilly pushed her aside roughly. 'Is it struck dumb, y'are?' he shouted, shaking the boy's head from side to side. 'Speak up now or I'll give you the

146

hiding the like of which the bloody Murdoch himself would envy!'

The rest of the gang had stopped their preparations for departure and were gathering round.

'What's up, Reilly?' Dodger wanted to know, his tone plainly disapproving. 'What's the poor little sod done to ye now?'

'I'll tell ye what he's done!' the Irishman raged. 'I jest heard him with me own two ears telling herself that he'd fixed it so she'd be free this very day, so I did!'

Several of the men laughed. 'Talk's cheap,' Dodger scoffed. 'Trying to make out he's a big man, that's all.'

'Don't let him gull ye, Reilly,' Sam put in. 'How the hell could he set her free without us seeing him?'

'I tell ye the young varmint's not to be trusted,' Reilly replied angrily. 'We'll not be safe till we're rid of him.'

'And if he don't consent to be got rid of?' Dodger enquired sarcastically. 'He'd lose us a sight quicker out here than we'd lose him.'

Reilly's eyes turned to the musket cradled in Dodger's arm. 'Oh, no ye don't!' the little Cockney exclaimed, drawing back a step. 'Hanging Murdoch's one thing but the kid's one of our mob. You ain't killing him jest 'cos ye heard him showing off to the woman.'

Muttered support came from the men. To their ignorant, superstitious minds Rob's ability to survive in the bush and to appear and disappear at will gave him a puckish quality which amused and scared them a little at the same time. In spite of his hatred of Rob, Reilly felt this no less than the others.

'Showing off, was it?' His anger and distrust subsided as he realised the practical impossibility of Rob's setting the hostages free. 'Well, that's as maybe but one thing's sure — he ain't coming no further with us.'

'Why not?' asked Sam.

'Cos I says so, that's why not!' Reilly snapped.

'How d'ye reckon ye'll stop him if he's a mind to follow us?' Dodger asked, grinning.

For answer, the man dragged Rob by the hair to the nearest tree and pushed him roughly against it. 'Gimme a rope,' he ordered. No one moved. 'Did ye not hear me? Gimme a rope,' he repeated, shouting.

Mandy confronted Reilly angrily. 'Would ye leave the laddie tied to a tree in this empty wilderness?' she demanded.

The Irishman glared at her. 'Is it shot dead ye'd have him then, is it? That's the way it would suit me but it's soft-hearted these are, all at once. This way he'll have the same chance as the blacksmith and that's more than he deserves, to be sure.'

Rob made no attempt to resist as he was bound to the tree. When the job was done, Reilly made a point of checking the knots. 'It's the wonder of the world ye'll be if ye can get out of that,' he remarked grimly as he hoisted himself into the saddle. 'If the good luck's with ye the troopers'll get to ye afore the ants do.'

Rob spoke for the first time. 'It's youse'll want the good luck, Reilly!' he shouted after him cheekily.

Reilly dug his heels savagely into his horse's flanks.

By the afternoon the going became rougher as they entered the hill country and Reilly was no longer concerned that his captives might try to gallop away over the rough ground. For the first time, the three found themselves able to talk freely. Mandy's thoughts were of Rob. 'I bade him take care but he would take no heed of me.'

'How could he have done anything to help us?' Prudence asked disdainfully 'He was pretending, just to show off. He can't be trusted, he's such a liar...'

'That will be enough, Miss Prudence!' Mandy rebuked her curtly. 'I dinna ken how ye can say such things with the poor laddie tied up all alone and smiling at us as we rode away.'

A sudden shout from Reilly diverted their attention. He had been riding with Sam at the head of the column; now he was stopped, one hand raised in warning.

The way ahead was blocked by armed Aborigines, fifty strong at least. From the rocks and trees on either side of them others were emerging until they were surrounded by a hundred or more black warriors watching them. Reilly and his men returned the silent inspection nervously.

Dodger cantered over to join Reilly and Sam. 'What's going on?' he enquired in an anxious voice. 'It's a cert they ain't come to share a billy of tea with us, all painted up with spears and shields. It means trouble, don't it, Reilly?'

149

Reilly made no reply. He was leaning forward and staring straight ahead, his eyes narrowed to mere slits.

'That bloody kid's with 'em!' he declared at last. 'It's himself standing there beside the big fella, Murringoo, their fight leader.'

'Then it's all right if the kid's with 'em,' Dodger remarked hopefully.

'I told ye the little sod was gulling us,' Reilly retorted. 'We should've finished him, like I said.'

Rob's voice rang out suddenly. 'We're coming to get ye, Reilly, if you don't let them three go!'

The tall black man beside Rob made a threatening gesture with his spear and the natives began to close in slowly.

'Let the woman and the kids go,' Dodger urged. 'I told ye we done wrong taking 'em in the first place.'

Reilly cocked his musket and raised it to his shoulder. 'Stop 'em!' he shouted. 'Ye hear me, Murringoo? Stop 'em where they are or I'll blow the boy's head off the way I should've back there!'

The slow, ominous advance continued unchecked.

'Put yer gun down, ye fool!' Sam cried. 'There's ten of them for every one of us!'

'Shut up!' Reilly snapped. 'Ye don't know these black heathens the way I do. One shot of a musket and they'll be off like the devil himself was after them.'

Rob and Murringoo were now well within musket range and still advancing.

'It's a last warning I'm giving ye!' Reilly yelled, an edge of fear to his voice in spite of his bold front. 'Stop where y'are or, so help me, I'll put a hole in his skull!'

The Irishman squeezed the trigger. A thunderous explosion rent the air as his head and shoulders disappeared in a ball of fire and smoke. His horse reared up, rolling him backwards out of the saddle as he dropped his gun and clutched at his face with both hands. He crashed to the ground and lay motionless beside the smoking remains of his musket, its muzzle split from end to end and bent like a giant horse shoe.

The Aboriginal warriors gave a great shout of triumph. Dodger and Sam controlled their own horses with difficulty as they stared in bewilderment at the still form of their leader.

'Bloody gun blew up in his face!' Dodger exclaimed. He swung his horse around to face the black army. 'Ye can have the woman!' he yelled. 'And the two kids. We won't stop ye!'

He was too late. The rest of the gang, now leaderless, panicked at the approach of the menacing spears and fired. The result was pandemonium. Gun after gun exploded and flew to pieces as the echoes rolled around the hills in relentless mockery.

Horses reared up, whinnying with terror and throwing their riders to the ground. Several lay where they fell, others scrambled to their feet and staggered about blindly, half stunned, faces burnt and streaming blood.

Only Sam and Dodger and a couple of others got away unscathed. Sensing danger in their own weapons, they had thrown them away and galloped off into the bush. The black advance had stopped. The native warriors were leaning on their spears, lost in wonder at the madness of the white men and the futility of their noisy firearms.

In the rear and away from the main action, Mandy and the children had managed to keep their own mounts under control but could not see everything that was going on. Suddenly Rob was with them. Beaming with delight, he caught Mandy as she slid from her horse.

'Rob!' she cried, hugging him. 'How did you get here? What was all that dreadful noise? What's going on?'

'Didn't I tell ye I'd have ye free today?' he replied gleefully. 'Didn't I tell ye?'

Mandy shrank away involuntarily as Murringoo strode up. He exchanged a few words in his own language with Rob, then turned away, waving his arms and shouting instructions to his followers.

Rob laughed at Mandy's nervousness. 'He won't harm ye,' he said. 'He's the boss man, a real gent. He's telling them to go home now, the fight's all over. Him and a couple of others are coming back with us to pick up their cant.'

Mandy's eyes followed the black fight leader as he walked away, tall, lithe and straight as one of his own spears. She began to understand Rob's admiration for the man and his people.

'He's coming back with us?' she asked. 'Why?'

'They was keeping jack on me all the time, see? Soon as youse lot left they had them ropes off of me. I promised them summat for helping. That's their cant. I reckon they earned it.'

152

'Aye,' Mandy agreed readily, 'they have earned a good reward.'

'And you will be rewarded, too,' Prudence declared. 'Papa will see to that.'

Rob looked the girl up and down coldly. 'I done it for her,' he said, indicating Mandy with a jerk of his thumb. 'Youse was just lucky ye was with her.'

'Nevertheless Papa will insist,' Prudence maintained almost humbly.

'I don't take nothink from no illegitimates,' Rob replied proudly. 'I'm currency, I am.'

'That will do, Rob,' Mandy chided him. 'There are men hurt. We must attend to them as best we can...'

Thomas took Rob by the arm. 'What did you do last night?' he asked, still bemused by the dramatic sequence of events. 'Was it you made all their guns blow up like that?'

'Course it was,' he replied cockily.

'But what exactly did you do?'

'I put stones in their guns and rammed 'em down with clay, see?'

Thomas regarded him with respectful wonder. 'I say! But how did you know it would work so well?'

'The doctor, he showed me how to load a musket,' Rob said knowingly. 'And how not to.'

'Come along, you two,' Mandy called. 'I need your help with these wounded men.'

Chapter 22

Ambush

Shortly before noon, Dr Middleton and the troopers reached the remains of the Weatherby homestead. Already order was emerging from the chaos left by Reilly's gang. Mr Weatherby had recovered from the shock of the attack and, stimulated by Morgan's energy and skills, was attending to the restoration of the house. Middleton was impatient to be gone. 'We are in need of food while our horses are refreshed. We can afford no more than an hour, then we must be on our way again.'

Now accompanied by Mr Weatherby, they camped that night well beyond the far boundary of the doctor's land. No skill was required to follow the fresh, well-trodden trail and only the failing light and their horses' need for rest halted them. At dawn they were off again.

'They can't be far ahead of us now,' Middleton observed as the sun rose clear of the trees. 'We might come upon them at any time.'

'They have no more than fifteen men, I think you said,' Captain Devereau observed thoughtfully.

'So far as we can judge,'

'We must be careful not to let them take us by surprise.'

They rode on in silence. The country was hilly now and the going becoming rougher. As they approached a sharp rise, the captain signalled his men to stop.

'I'm going to the top of the ridge ahead of us to see what lies on the other side,' he explained to the sergeant. 'You and your men will wait here and keep your eyes open.' He turned to Middleton and Weatherby. 'I should like you to come with me. You know this country; I don't.'

The three men approached the crest of the ridge on their stomachs. At the top the captain peered cautiously through the tall grass. 'Good God!' he breathed, beckoning the other two to join him. They all stared in astonishment at the sheep and cows scattered over the gully beneath them, grazing hungrily and apparently untended.

'Either they've abandoned the animals or they're uncommon careless,' Devereau said. 'Unless, as I rather suspect, we're being led into a trap.' He drew out a small telescope from a leather cylinder attached to his belt and focussed it on the scene below. After a few moments he handed the telescope to Middleton.

'I see a campfire...' The doctor paused, concentrating. '...It can't be! But, by heaven, it is! Mandy, Prudence and Thomas! All active and free and apparently unharmed!'

Weatherby snatched the instrument from him. 'Heaven be praised! They're alive!' he exclaimed. 'But there are men there, too.'

He passed the telescope back to the captain and they waited for his opinion of the strange scene. 'You're right,' he said. 'I can make out nine but there

155

may be more. Some appear to have their heads bandaged and others are asleep. We must treat this as a trap. With all those animals to hold them back they must have realised they would soon be overtaken. An ambush would be their only chance.'

Middleton agreed. 'When Reilly planned this devilment, he was counting on taking my horses and leaving us stranded. That would have given him time to get well away into the hills before we could have got help...'

A slight sound from the trees at their side made them turn quickly. Standing watching them were four black men, armed with spears, clubs and shields, their bodies painted with yellow and white shapes resembling dappled sun light. They stood still as painted ebony statues, their eyes almost hidden by dark, shaggy brows. From ground level they looked very tall and menacing.

A burst of boyish laughter came from the thick scrub beneath the trees as Rob slithered down the steep, grassy slope towards the group of Aborigines. He jumped to his feet as he reached the side of the tallest of the four men. 'Give ye a fright, did they?' he grinned.

'So this is your doing, Rob? I should have known.' There was relief in the doctor's voice. 'And these men are friends of yours, I take it?'

Rob watched the three white men as they scrambled to their feet feeling rather foolish. 'They won't harm ye,' he assured them. 'It was them as saved Miss and the two kids.' He looked up with affectionate pride at the tall black man beside him. 'This 'un's Murringoo. He's the boss man. I told him ye'd be sure to give him summat for their help, so him and these other three is coming back with us.'

'But those men were armed with muskets,' Middleton said. 'And yet your black friends...'

The boy smiled. 'I fixed their guns, see? I plugged 'em with stones and clay like you said not to when you learned me to load, so when they fired 'em they blowed up like you said.' He laughed merrily at the recollection. 'Some of 'em got away but I don't reckon they'll make any more flummut for ye.'

'So that's why those men are lying down there with their heads bandaged?'

Rob nodded. 'Miss patched 'em up like but you best take a look at 'em.'

The doctor checked the men's injuries. One had already died, others, including Reilly, were close to death.

'Will he live?' Mandy asked as they knelt beside the Irishman.

'I doubt if he will survive the return journey, which is perhaps just as well for him.'

As they stood up, Captain Devereau approached. 'May I speak to you, sir? Alone,' he added with a glance at Mandy. They walked away together, the captain plainly worried.

'A damnably awkward situation has arisen,' he began. 'My sergeant tells me that the tall native leader has a price on his head.'

Middleton frowned. 'What makes him think that?'

'He says a black man answering to his description is wanted for the murder of a settler at a place called Patrick Plains a year ago. He seems quite convinced of it.'

'But we only have the sergeant's word for it,' the doctor pointed out. 'Does he know the man personally? Has he ever seen him before?'

'No, but he claims that the printed description posted in the barracks at Wallis Plains fits the man perfectly.'

'Damnation! We can't possibly arrest the fellow! He's just done us a service of inestimable value. We are deeply in his debt. To arrest him would be unthinkable. Tell your sergeant he must forget the whole matter.'

'I'm afraid he would never agree to that. Apart from any considerations of justice, there is a reward...'

'I'll pay him his reward! I don't care how much it is. Tell him to come to me. I'm the local civil magistrate.'

'One way around the difficulty occurs to me, if you are agreeable,' Devereau went on. 'We could postpone the actual arrest until we get back to the Weatherby's...' He raised a hand as the doctor prepared to protest. 'Please hear me out. It may not come to that. This lad, Rob, apparently speaks the native tongue so on the return journey he can talk to the man, discover his whereabouts at the time of the murder, perhaps establish his innocence beyond doubt. We could then refuse to arrest him on the grounds of mistaken identity.'

Middleton shook his head vigorously. 'No, no, no! One word of this to Rob and we would lose him instantly. His loyalty to his black friends is greater than his loyalty to us, make no mistake about that!'

'But the boy is white. Surely he feels a closer kinship with his own people?'

'His own people,' Middleton repeated bitterly. 'What have his own people ever done to him except drive his mother to suicide then try to starve him, beat him and drive him away? It was the blacks who made him welcome, accepted him as one of their own, shared their food with him, taught him how to survive in the wild and gave him their trust. No, no! Arrest his friend, Murringoo, and you will have every black man in the valley on our backs! There would never be peace in the valley again!'

'Then what in heaven's name am I to tell the sergeant?'

'There is nothing we can do at present. Tell your sergeant the matter is being looked into carefully by me, a magistrate, and that I will see justice is done and that he receives any reward he may be entitled to. Our first duty, tell him, is to these wounded men. By the time we have reached Weatherby's place a solution may have occurred to one of us. In the meantime, captain, please instruct your men to keep this strictly to themselves.'

'So be it,' Devereau agreed with a shrug.

That night Reilly died along with two more of his men. They were buried side by side near the track which was to have been their road to freedom and a cairn of rocks set up to mark the spot.

On the second day, as they approached the Weatherby homestead, Rob and Thomas galloped ahead with the glad tidings. Thomas rushed into the partially restored house to find his mother as Rob tumbled excitedly from his horse into Morgan's arms.

'Ye don't need to wait no longer, Morgan!' he cried. 'Miss is here! I brung her back safe!'

159

'Those villains never harmed her?' Morgan demanded, his hands crushing the boy's shoulders.

Rob laughed. 'No bloody fear! I had me eye on her all the time. Murringoo and me, we kept jack on her. If one of them sods had touched her he'd have got a spear through his guts, I tell ye!'

The tension in the man's hand relaxed. 'You did well, boyo! Oh, you did well!' There were tears in his eyes as he shook the boy gently. 'I'll never be out of your debt, look you, not if I live to be a hundred!'

When the main party arrived and Morgan was lifting Mandy down from her high seat on the wagon, Rob pulled urgently at his loose smock-like shirt. 'Now's yer chance, Morgan! Now!' he urged in a hoarse whisper.

The blacksmith's response as he gently set Mandy on her feet was a fierce warning glare that would have melted one of his own horseshoes. Rob walked away, shaking his head in despair at his hero's cowardice.

Mandy hid a smile. 'Thank ye, Mr Jones,' she said with quiet formality, her innocent blue eyes gazing steadily into his until he was forced to look down in embarrassment. She turned to go but his voice, breathless as if he had been running, stopped her. She waited. 'Aye, Mr Jones?'

Morgan looked hopelessly from side to side, seeing nothing of the bustling activity all around them — not even Rob, regarding them both dolefully as he helped unharness the bullock team. 'Aye, Mr Jones?' Mandy repeated. The hint of impatience in her voice brought the big man back to earth. His Adam's apple bobbed as he swallowed to moisten his dry throat.

'Mistress McInnes,' he began with a mighty effort. 'I'm a plain man and a simple one without means nor education as none knows better than yourself so I have little hope that you should ever notice me with favour...' He broke off suddenly, lips dry and cheeks flaming.

'It would be hard not to notice ye, with or without favour, Mr Jones,' Mandy remarked kindly. 'But I canna be standing here talking to ye when I should be waiting on poor Mrs Weatherby.'

Mention of Mrs Weatherby and the recollection of Mandy's patient acceptance of that lady's snobbery and abuse released in Morgan a desperate courage. 'Damn Mrs Weatherby!' he exclaimed. 'Rob is right; you are too good a woman to be wasted on such as her!'

Mandy smiled. 'Do ye have some other employment to offer me then, Mr Jones?'

'Yes, indeed!' he replied eagerly. 'If you will pardon the boldness and be good enough not to laugh ...' He took a deep breath. '... I would ask your hand in marriage...' He stared down at her, a terrified giant ready to flee.

The smile faded from Mandy's lips as she looked up into the man's pathetically earnest face. She raised a hand and touched his curly beard tenderly.

'Ye're a fine man, Morgan Jones,' she said with deep sincerity. 'I take it most kindly that ye should wish to wed me and I am nothing displeased by the notion.'

161

Before Morgan could think of anything to say, she was hurrying away. He stood, mouth agape, following her with unbelieving eyes, hope welling within him. Suddenly Rob was at his side, angry and contemptuous. 'I seen her go off,' he said, deep scorn in his voice. 'Ye're a glocky fool, Morgan! I give up on ye!'

He turned to walk away but the man's strong hand grasped his shoulder and swung him around. Rob glared at him defiantly. Morgan was still gazing wide-eyed at Mandy's retreating form like a man who had just witnessed a miracle. 'I did it, boyo!' he whispered incredulously. 'I did it, look you!'

Chapter 23

Murringoo

The success of the rescue was marred for Dr Middleton by the unsolved problem of Murringoo. The sergeant's certainty that he was the wanted man could not be shaken and, as Captain Devereau was restless to return to Wallis Plains with his prisoners, a decision had to be made quickly. Morgan was in no doubt about the best thing to do. 'Don't arrest him, sir, whatever you do,' he recommended promptly when the doctor sought his advice. 'There must be a way around it, you being a Justice of the Peace and all.'

'Aren't you forgetting one thing, Morgan? The man may be a murderer.'

'Then he's paid for it three times over by what he's done since,' Morgan argued warmly. 'He saved the lives of Mistress McInnes and the two children, look you.'

Middleton sighed. 'Privately, I agree with you. For myself, I shouldn't hesitate but unfortunately there are others involved. The sergeant is set on getting his reward and the captain must do his duty. And so, it seems, must I for, as a magistrate, I am sworn to uphold the law.'

'Then send him away, sir. Send him packing before anyone has the chance to arrest him. Rob can explain the reason to him in his own tongue. He can tell him to go away and come back later when the troopers have gone.'

The doctor's spirits rose. Such a direct and simple solution had not occurred to him. He sent for Rob at once.

'Morgan and I want you to do something very important for us,' he began as the boy entered. 'We want you to do it now, and quickly, with no questions asked. It concerns your friend, Murringoo.'

Rob regarded the two men with the cool glint of distrust in his eyes.

'We want you to send Murringoo away.'

'Why?'

'No questions, Rob, please.'

'But what about his cant? Ye ain't give him nothink for what he done back there so why d'ye want him to go away?'

'There is no time now for gifts. Believe me, Rob, this is for his own good. He can come later for his reward.'

'Why?'

The doctor looked at Morgan and gave a hopeless shrug. Morgan turned to Rob and spoke seriously. 'Now you listen to me, boyo, that friend of yours is wanted for murder of a white man and the captain will have to arrest him. You don't want that now, do you?'

The boy's eyes blazed. 'He never done no wrong! That white scum took his woman and when he'd done with her he killed her so Murringoo went

164

after him and killed him. That's the blacks' law, that is. What's wrong with it?'

Middleton looked away uncomfortably. He knew only too well that if Murringoo were tried the death sentence would be a foregone conclusion. No black man would be allowed to get away with killing a white, no matter what the provocation. The tragedy was that according to the ancient tribal laws that Murringoo understood, thousands of years older than the laws the white man had brought with him, he had simply righted a wrong in the only way acceptable to his own people.

Without another word, Rob ran from the hut. Murringoo and his three companions had settled themselves on a slope overlooking the homestead. Here, beneath a fragile bark shelter, they sat cross-legged, totally absorbed in the fascinating show provided by the white men. Rob flopped to the ground and breathlessly explained the threat to Murringoo's life. Silently the four men rose, gathered their weapons and slipped away into the bush. Rob stood for a moment, watching them out of sight then walked slowly back to Morgan who was cutting turf for the homestead's roof.

'They gone, boyo?' he asked quietly. Rob nodded. 'That's an end to that then,' Morgan said, plainly relieved.

He was wrong. Half an hour later the sergeant and three troopers rode up to the captain's tent. Beside the sergeant's horse stumbled Murringoo, his wrists tied behind his back and a leading rope around his neck.

Devereau emerged from the tent and regarded the scene with a puzzled frown. 'What's the

165

meaning of this, sergeant?' he asked, trying to conceal his displeasure.

The sergeant saluted. 'Caught him trying to run away, sir, but I had my eye on him.'

Devereau thought hard. 'You did well, sergeant,' he forced himself to say.

'Best get leg irons on him, sir,' the sergeant advised. 'They're tricky devils, these Injuns.'

'Yes, yes, of course. I shall see to it.'

When Morgan was given the task of riveting the iron bands around Murringoo's ankles, he called on Rob for assistance. At first the boy refused to help and agreed only after Morgan pointed out it would give him a good chance to talk to his friend.

'What'll I tell him?' Rob asked miserably. 'He ain't glocky. Now they got him he knows they'll hang him.'

'It's not like you to give up so easy, boyo,' Morgan chided him. 'Where there's a will there's a way, my old mam used to say.' Rob looked sharply at his friend, a sudden hope revived by the cheerful note in his voice. 'There's a trick of the blacksmith's trade I've yet to teach you,' Morgan went on, 'and now is as good a time as any for you to learn it.'

Morgan picked up a pair of leg-irons, two small hoops of iron connected by a short length of chain. The hoops were open so they could be slipped around the prisoner's ankles and the open ends brought together under pressure and riveted. 'Sit down and hold your foot up,' Morgan ordered.

Rob dropped to the ground and extended one bare foot, his eyes bright with interest. The blacksmith fitted one of the iron bands around the outstretched ankle and the great muscles of his arms

166

bunched as he squeezed the open ends together with his bare hands.

'Try to pull your foot out of that, boyo.'

Rob struggled to free his foot but the ring of iron was too small.

Morgan nodded, smiling. 'That's because it's round, look you, but if I was to hammer the sides closer together and make it egg-shaped, it would be a different matter.' Rob looked doubtful. 'Take my word for it, boyo. It's a trick I learned in Sydney town from the old lags. They call it "ovalling".' He gazed steadily into the boy's eyes. 'You take my meaning now?' A smile of understanding spread over the boy's face. He nodded. 'There's clever you are then.' The powerful hands grasped the ends of the iron band and in a moment it was open again. Rob scrambled to his feet.

'When you going to do it?' he asked.

'Not me, boyo.'

'Who then?'

'You. It'd be more than my ticket-of-leave was worth if I was caught at it.'

The boy considered for a moment. 'Tonight, eh?' Morgan nodded. 'But the hammer'll sing out, won't it?'

'Muffle the hammer with a piece of old blanket. Anything will do.'

That night, Thomas, sleeping alone in a tent while the house was being made habitable again, was awakened by a gentle shake. 'Ye got to help me set Murringoo free,' he heard Rob whisper.

'Does Dr Middleton know?'

'No, but if he did he'd be glad of it. Stands to reason, don't it?

A pause. 'Well, what do you want me to do this time?'

Rob explained, 'They got him roped to a post, see, with leg-irons on him. And there's a so'jer keeping jack on him and I can't do nothink with him there so you got to get him away, see?'

'But how?'

'Easy! All ye got to do is just walk out there in yer nightshirt like you was asleep.'

'You mean, pretend to be sleep-walking?'

'Ye can do it easy! He'll see ye and come after ye. It's a fakement, see, like before.'

Thomas rose from his straw-filled mattress on the ground. 'But how can you get the leg-irons off?' he wanted to know.

Rob pulled him towards the tent flap. 'I fixed them bloody muskets, didn't I? Come on!'

Together they slipped away, Thomas's long nightshirt glowing ghostly white in the pale light of a half moon.

When the trooper guarding Murringoo first noticed the spectral figure of Thomas floating slowly past he was gripped by such superstitious terror that he was barely able to remain at his post. Slowly reason began to return and, as his brain thawed out, he decided that this was no supernatural spirit but an ordinary human being in a white nightshirt. Someone was walking in his sleep. The Weatherby boy, most likely. His vigilance, he felt sure, would not go unrewarded if he conducted the sleepwalker back to the safety of the house. He glanced at his prisoner, crouched beside the thick wooden post to which he was tied like a dog on a short lead. He could be safely left unguarded for a few minutes. As the trooper trotted off after Thomas, Rob appeared from the shadows. Murringoo grunted his surprise. The boy waited till Thomas and the soldier were out of sight and then went to work, first slashing at the ropes binding the man's hands and freeing him from the post. Murringoo was on his feet now. Rob pulled at one of his feet until the iron band around his ankle was hard against the base of the post. The first blow of the muffled hammer sounded to Rob's taut nerves loud enough to wake everyone within half a mile. But there was no stopping now. Rob could feel the iron band yielding with each blow. It was easier than he had expected. He dropped the hammer, lifted the man's foot and dragged roughly at the partially flattened band.

Murringoo remained stoically silent as the skin of his heel was raked by the rough edge of the leg-iron. His blood, warm and slippery, acted as a lubricant. Slowly the iron ring was forced down over the foot until, to Rob's great joy, it slid off in his hands. The second leg-iron was easier now that Murringoo knew what was required of him. As the hammer rose and fell again, Rob was acutely aware that one badly aimed blow could smash the man's ankle. Two minutes later Murringoo was a free man.

Rob stood up and thrust the knife and hammer into his friend's hands. 'For you,' he gasped in the native language. 'Keep them. A gift. Later I will bring you much more. Go now — quickly!'

Breathless, sweating and filled with relief, he watched the black man disappear. He was about to turn and run when a firm hand seized his arm.

Twisting around, he found himself face to face with Captain Devereau.

'Where is the captive?' Devereau demanded.

'Gone!' Rob replied defiantly. 'I took the leg-irons off of him!'

'What have you done with the man on guard?'

'He ain't hurt.'

Devereau's grip on his arm relaxed slightly. 'So no one knows about this but you and me?' he asked quietly.

Before Rob could answer, the captain's body jerked forward, his knees buckled under him and he collapsed face down into the grass. The boy stared aghast at the prone form. From a small cut in the back of the captain's tunic a patch of blood was spreading a dark stain in the moonlight.

Murringoo wiped the blade of the knife Rob had given him. The boy waved urgently, for him to be gone. As the black figure merged again with the shadows under the trees, Rob stared in near panic at the still body at his feet. He had not expected an outcome like this. There was no other way for him now; he had to disappear too, but first he must fetch the doctor. He looked up quickly. The guard was returning, whistling softly to himself, happily unaware of what had been going on in his brief absence. Rob backed away and followed Murringoo into the trees. The guard would quickly have the doctor on the scene.

Chapter 24

The Old Bailey

Murringoo's wounding of Captain Devereau was serious but not fatal, thanks to the Englishman's robust constitution and Dr Middleton's prompt attention. The captain's tent had been converted into a sick bay and Jake Brightwell, now one of the doctor's trusties, had been relieved of all other work to look after him, day and night.

Murringoo and Rob had vanished with the rest of the Aboriginal tribe. The sergeant and his men spent several wet and miserable days scouring the district but it was as though they had never existed. Finally, the search was abandoned and a very frustrated sergeant left with his men and their convict prisoners for the barracks at Wallis Plains. Mandy and Morgan were relieved to see them go. Their only regret was that they didn't expect to see Rob again for he would surely have a price on his head, too, and had most likely gone to live with his Aboriginal friends permanently. Officially, Dr Middleton's duty was clear: as the local magistrate he must now order not only Murringoo's arrest but Rob's as well if they should ever come back into the district again.

The departure of the troopers was no less a relief to Captain Devereau, who was glad to be free of any military duties. It was arranged that as soon as he was well enough to travel, Morgan would take him to Newcastle and put him on the boat for Sydney. There he would present the Governor with a report on the whole affair as well as a letter from Dr Middleton, recommending Mandy's release from Mrs Weatherby's service in order to marry Morgan. Quite a time might have to pass before this happy event could take place. In the meantime Mandy continued to work for the Weatherbys and an extra duty now was helping Jake to look after the captain. 'And how is the captain today?' Mr Weatherby asked as she returned from a dash to his tent in the continuing rain.

Mandy hung up her cape and pulled off her wet boots. 'Very much better, sir, I believe. He has more colour to his cheeks and his spirits seem much improved. I think he finds Jake Brightwell's company quite agreeable.'

'Stuff and nonsense!' Mrs Weatherby exclaimed. 'How could a gentleman such as he, the son of Viscount Woodbridge of Manningtree, have anything in common with that convict person?'

'They seem to have much to talk about, m'am.'

Mrs Weatherby sighed deeply. 'If only it had been possible for us to accommodate him in our own house, I'm sure he would have found our conversation a great deal more interesting and elevating, poor man!'

Elevating the captain might have found the good lady's conversation but, to judge by his

172

attention as Jake answered the questions he put to him, hardly more interesting.

'Maggie Jackson, mister? Oh, ah. I mind her well. We come out on the same ship, ye see. Over thirteen years gone now it was. Another few months and I'll have done me time.' He wagged his head and winked. 'I'll be a clean potato then — a real Botany Bay swell!'

Devereau smiled. 'But tell me more about this Maggie Jackson, Jake. What did she look like? What sort of young woman would you say she was?'

'Oh, a real sight for sore eyes was Maggie', Jake replied feelingly. 'As pretty a piece as ever I seen in my life, she was. Nothing flashy about her but she weren't no cheap judy, neither. She were a real square rigger, if ye ask me.'

'You mean she was not like the other female convicts? A cut above them — something of a lady, perhaps?'

'That's what I just said, weren't it?'

The captain nodded. 'How old would you say she was?'

'She was a close 'un, was Maggie. She never let on nothink about herself but I reckon she was... nigh about twenty.'

'And her boy, Rob? He was born on the voyage, I believe?'

'Aye. I mind it well. She had a hard time of it, so the women said. Lucky, she was to come through with herself and the babby alive, they reckon.'

'Tell me, Jake; why did she kill herself?'

'It was that bloody Factory done it... The Women's Factory at Parramatta, mister. The House of Correction for Females — that's its proper handle.' Jake sniffed derisively. 'House of Correction, says you? House of Iniquity, more like, says I!'

'So she didn't like the Factory?'

'No bloody fear! They made her life hell. She could have had the pick of the officers of the garrison, could Maggie, but she wouldn't look at none of 'em. Them other women was jealous of her, see? Jealous of her soft way of talking, even the way she looked after that damn kid. And one day she couldn't take it no longer and when the river was in high flood she made an end of herself.'

'Yet the boy survived.'

'Swimming, he was, mister! Paddling along like a little dog when the ferryman hooked him out, then he ups and offs into the woods without so much as a by-your-leave and he weren't seen again for a twelvemonth or more. He'd been living with the blacks, ye see, and he's been living with 'em off and on ever since.' Jake paused and looked shrewdly at the captain. 'He'd never let you hang that Murringoo. Been like hanging his own brother.'

'What was his mother's crime, Jake?'

'Crime, mister?' The convict's eyebrows shot up in surprise. 'All ye brings with ye when ye're sent to Botany Bay is yer name, yer age and the term of yer sentence. Nothink else, mister. The Governor hisself don't know what ye done.'

Devereau regarded the convict doubtfully. 'You mean to say that if I asked the Governor in Sydney the nature of the crime committed by Maggie Jackson he would have no true record of it? No name of her accuser or any other circumstances of the case?'

'That's right. There's only two coves in the world could tell you that. The clerk of the court at the Old Bailey in London is one...'

'And the other?'

'Me, mister.'

'You, Jake?' the captain asked in astonishment. 'Why you?'

'Cos I went up with her at the Old Bailey. I seen the case they made out agin her... It were nowt, mister. A plain little gold ring what they reckoned she hooked from some highty-tighty old haybag of a toff as she was maid to. No more'n two bob's worth and they done her in for it!'

The captain had raised himself onto an elbow and was looking at the convict with rapt interest. 'And the name of this old... old toff, Jake? Do you remember her name?'

'Her?' he retorted bitterly. 'She never come into it. Them sort of people put ye in quick as look but they make bloody sure their own names don't get called out. No bloody fear!'

'But did you not see the woman who made the accusation, Jake?'

'I told ye! She kep' well out of it. She had some lawyer fella speak for her. Him in the white wig and the black dress. He reckoned Maggie lifted the ring and ran off with it and the peelers picked her up with it somewheres. I never told this to a living soul before, mister, strike me dead!'

There followed a long silence in the tent backed by the hypnotic drumming of rain on the taut canvas. Through the half open flap, the captain's eyes were fixed on the grey, rain-shrouded hills across the valley but his thoughts were half a world away.

'Youse a London man yerself, mister?' Jake ventured.

'Eh?' Devereau looked at Jake as though surprised to find he was not alone. 'A London man?' he repeated, gathering his scattered thoughts. 'Well, no, not really. More of a Norwich man. I have a friend — a very dear friend — who lives not far from Norwich, just out of Yarville.'

'Ah, Yarville!' Jake mused wistfully. 'I mind it well. A grand place for oysters, is Yarville.'

Chapter 25

The Earl

The big mail coach clattered over the rough stony road from Norwich to Yarville on the coast of Norfolk. On an outside seat, well muffled against the chill morning air of an English spring, Captain Devereau braced himself against the lurching of the vehicle, ducking to avoid the switching fingers of the roadside oaks which whipped at him as the coach sped past. From his high seat he could see for miles across the flat countryside through the skeleton trees now flecked with green buds. What a contrast to the New South Wales landscape he had left six months before, he reflected. It would be autumn in the Hunter valley now but the gum trees would still be grey-green and leafy as ever. He hunched his shoulders and drew the wide collar of his greatcoat up around his ears to protect them from the cold rush of the air. The action made him think of Rob, living naked in the bush with his Aboriginal friends... The coachman's horn blared cheerfully, announcing their arrival at the outskirts of Yarville. The roadside trees had given way to tiny brick and timber cottages with thick, thatched roofs and soon they would pull up in the yard of an old hotel, The Duke's Head where he would hire a saddle horse to carry him the few miles further up the coast.

The captain's destination was a brick castle, complete with moat and drawbridge, built nearly five hundred years ago by one of Henry V's generals who had lifted a fortune in booty from the unlucky French after the battle of Agincourt, but it was a later king who had bestowed on the general's descendants the earldom of Yarville.

In the central courtyard of the castle an ostler took his horse. He climbed a short flight of worn stone steps, tugged at a rusty iron bell-pull beside the door and waited. The heavy door swung slowly open and the butler, in velvet knee breeches, gave the visitor a cool, appraising look before breaking into a delighted smile of recognition. 'Captain Charles!' he greeted him cordially. 'His Lordship will be pleased! He is in the library. I will announce you at once, sir.'

The Earl of Yarville, seated before a stone fireplace that seemed to occupy most of one wall, looked up, frowning as though displeased by the unexpected intrusion. He was a comparatively young man in his mid-thirties but his dark, wavy hair, already greying at the temples, and a severe, unsmiling mouth, gave him the look of an older man. He waited for the butler to speak.

'A gentleman to see you, milord. Captain the Honourable Charles Devereau...'

As the earl stood up and turned, his face was transformed by a heart-warming smile of welcome. 'Charles! I don't believe it!' He embraced his friend then held him at arm's length as he gazed earnestly into his eyes. 'My dear fellow, why didn't you write to warn me? Your last letter from New South Wales gave no hint of your returning so soon.'

'There seemed little point in writing when I should most likely have been a passenger on the same ship as my letter,' Devereau replied lightly. He dropped into a leather chesterfield and leaned forward, hands extended to the fire. The earl sat down beside him.

'What news from New South Wales, Charles? You've seen the Governor and discussed our proposal with him?'

'Yes, oh yes... But we'll talk about that later, if you don't mind. I want to talk to you — and very seriously — but not about land in the meantime.'

'By all means, let us talk,' the earl agreed as he resumed his seat. 'But about what?'

The captain stared into the flames to avoid his friend's puzzled eyes. 'I'm not sure how to tell you about this,' he began. 'You see, the last thing I want to do is to raise your hopes and see them dashed again...'

'For heaven's sake, man, out with it!'

'Don't be shocked, Rob, but this may concern Margaret.'

'Margaret?' the earl repeated incredulously. 'Margaret? My wife?'

As briefly as he could, the captain related what he knew of Maggie Jackson's history.

'But there must be countless Margaret Jacksons in the world,' his friend responded uneasily. 'Jackson is not an uncommon name. Surely you aren't seriously suggesting...?'

Devereau turned to look steadily into his companion's eyes for the first time. He reached out

179

and took his hand and held it. 'Rob, there is one other fact I have to tell you. This particular girl was sentenced at the Old Bailey fourteen years ago at the same time as Margaret disappeared. There are other coincidences too great to be ignored. They have to be thoroughly investigated.'

'But the idea is preposterous! In any case, how does one investigate such matters?'

'The only detailed records are in London with the clerk of the court at the Old Bailey. I have no right to pry into them without your consent.'

He saw the pain in the man's eyes and went on in a softer voice. 'You see, Rob, if this Maggie Jackson should, by some miracle, turn out to be the girl you married, then you have a son and heir in New South Wales.'

The earl closed his eyes and was silent for a long time. 'Haven't you overlooked one important fact?' he said at last, controlling his voice with a great effort. 'Jackson was Margaret's maiden name. When we were married she became Margaret Preston.'

'But your marriage was a secret, Rob — a secret from the family and particularly from your mother. Do you really believe she would have betrayed that secret without your consent, even to save her very life?'

There was another long silence. 'This convict you talked with, did he tell you what the girl looked like?'

'Jake wasn't the most articulate of men,' Devereau replied, 'but, certainly, from his description it could well have been Margaret.'

180

'And what crime was she supposed to have committed?'

'We can only discover that from the official record but Jake told me it was a matter of some petty theft...'

The earl rounded on his friend in sudden anger. 'Dammit, Charles! It is unthinkable! Margaret had no need to steal. She was incapable of such a thing! In any case, mother would never have allowed her to be charged and certainly never to be transported!' He rose abruptly and strode across the room to stand quite still, looking out through a tall, mullioned window. 'My mother was very fond of Margaret,' he went on, his anger subsiding a little. 'She was the daughter of mother's personal maid who married our head gardener, Jack Jackson. I don't need to remind you of that. And when Margaret's mother died, my mother made herself responsible for her welfare.'

Devereau seized the opportunity to take up the story. 'And when Margaret was sixteen or seventeen years old and you and your brothers began to notice she was a damned pretty girl and growing into a beautiful young woman, what happened? Suddenly your mother stopped treating her like a daughter. You told me so yourself. Suddenly Margaret became a servant — an upper servant but a servant nevertheless.'

'Mother made Margaret her personal companion. She wanted Margaret near her.'

'Quite!' the captain retorted. 'She wanted her where she could keep a close eye on her.' He joined his friend at the window. 'Listen to me, Rob. We mustn't fall out over this but I came to know your mother even better, perhaps, than you did. She was a proud, ambitious lady, even a ruthless one where her three sons were concerned. She had great plans for you all. She would have even considered it her duty to choose your wives if she had lived long enough. Your mother would have gone to any lengths to prevent one of her sons marrying the daughter of her head gardener.'

They stood side by side, silently gazing out over the castle gardens and the flat Norfolk countryside beyond. 'We all knew that,' Devereau went on relentlessly, 'you, Margaret and I. We knew that if your mother had suspected for one moment that you and Margaret were planning to marry, she would have done anything to prevent it.' He broke off, afraid of what he was about to say — 'even to having her sent far away to New South Wales if she could find no other way...' He waited, expecting an explosion but none came. 'We were told Margaret had run away to London and couldn't be found,' he continued, 'but we knew something that they didn't. We knew that you and she were married so why in heaven's name would she run away?'

The earl closed his eyes and groaned softly as Devereau continued, his voice softening. 'It's all long past now, Rob. It's the present and the living we must think of and the possibility that you may have a fourteen year old child — Margaret's son — in New South Wales.'

His companion wiped his wet cheeks with the back of his hand. 'Yes, yes, but you have had months to get used to the idea that Margaret may have been the victim of a damnable conspiracy. You've had

182

time to come to terms with it. I haven't. But I can see... Oh, I *know* that it's possible.' His voice broke. 'But if it is true, why didn't Margaret get in touch with me?'

'I'm sure she tried, Rob... But how? She would have been treated as a convicted felon. Any letter she wrote would have been ignored or destroyed but even if a letter had reached England do you suppose for one moment that your mother would have allowed you to receive it?'

Chapter 26

Official Records

A seedy little records clerk beneath the Old Bailey courthouse in London was reduced to a state of pathetic servility when he found himself faced with the Earl of Yarville and Captain Devereau. 'A great honour, milord! A great honour to serve you,' he chattered, beads of nervous perspiration breaking out on his forehead. 'Fourteen years ago, I believe Your Lordship said?... Yes, yes! To be sure! A very great honour! Follow me, milord.'

The clerk led them down into a musty basement, a depressing catacomb of a place, ill-lit, cobwebbed and lined with wooden shelves on which were piled the leather-bound court records going back centuries. It took him some time to find the great book in which his visitors were interested. He dragged it out, opened it at random and slammed it shut again to rid it of the dust of years. The earl sneezed, setting the timid little man into a nervous frenzy of apologies. The dust settled and the book was opened again with care. 'And the name of the party Your Lordship wishes to make enquiries of is...?' The clerk looked up over his small round spectacles with an interest his air of humility could not hide.

Devereau pressed a half sovereign into his hand. 'Leave us now, if you please,' he said. 'We shall call you if we need your help.'

In the dim light from a narrow, iron-barred window set high in the stone wall, the earl's face seemed to be drained of colour. 'You search, Charles,' he said and stood, looking up at the window as if in silent prayer.

The captain turned the crackling pages carefully, running a finger down the lists of cases until he stopped at the entry he was seeking yet dreading to find. He read silently, hunched over the wavy vellum page covered with ornate, spidery writing already beginning to fade.

JACKSON, Margaret Ann, spinster, maidservant of Yarville which is in Norfolk. Charged with GRAND LARCENY in that she did steal a Gold Ring of value greater than Two Shillings.

Spinster ... Devereau repeated the word to himself. She had kept her secret to the last, just as he knew she would. And the gold ring? Her own wedding ring most likely, which she wore on a ribbon around her neck since she dared not wear it on her finger. He read the account of the case to the end while his friend stood, hands clasped behind him, staring up at the prison-like window.

'It's all here,' Devereau said quietly at last. 'I'm sorry, Rob! It's all here, just as I feared. Your mother's name was kept out of it and no Yarville people were involved. She must have been brought up here to London on some pretext while you were away and... and just disappeared, a supposed runaway, which we know couldn't possibly have been the truth.'

The earl's face was haggard as he turned to face his companion. 'If I had only known! Oh, God, Charles! If I had only known she was carrying my child I would have spoken out and damn the family and my inheritance and all my mother's plans!'

Devereau closed the book with a sigh. 'We did what we both thought was best at the time. I was as much to blame as you for keeping the marriage a secret.' He placed a firm hand on his friend's back and steered him towards the door.

'We shall leave for New South Wales as soon as it is convenient for you,' the earl announced. 'If Margaret's grave can be found I shall bring her remains back here to be placed in the family vault. And we shall find my son and I shall devote the rest of my life to making his as rewarding as Margaret would have wished.' He tried to control the eagerness which had crept into his voice. 'Describe him to me, Charles. What sort of a boy is he?'

The captain's eyes glowed with a mischievous pleasure. He tried not to smile too broadly as he recalled his last encounter with the future Earl of Yarville.

Chapter 27

Government Business

Morgan stood over his anvil, hammer poised, listening. A drop of sweat ran off the end of his nose and fell with a fierce hiss on the red hot horseshoe he was fashioning. Horsemen were approaching. He put the hammer down and wiped his face with a towel then walked slowly towards the little white-washed cottage, shading his eyes as he gazed down the well-worn roadway. There were four riders and a packhorse and one of the riders was galloping ahead.

Mandy was standing in the cottage doorway, broom in hand. 'Who d'ye suppose these might be?' she asked, anxiety in her voice.

'They're not in uniform so they can't be troopers,' Morgan said.

'And a good thing, too! I'd not want to go through that again.'

There was something familiar about the leading horseman as he reined in and jumped lightly to the ground. Morgan recognised him with a glow of pleasure that quickly turned to apprehension. Mandy recognised him at the same time and two little worry lines creased her brow as Captain Devereau strode towards them. He approached smiling broadly, hand extended. His hope of finding Rob was centred on these two. 'Don't you remember me?' he asked, a little put out by the unexpected coolness of his reception.

Morgan took his outstretched hand and shook it dutifully. 'We weren't thinking to see you again, sir, not for a long time,' he replied. His words lacked cordiality. The captain turned expectantly to Mandy but she made no offer to shake his hand. He suddenly felt uncomfortable and unwelcome.

The three other riders, two of whom kept in the background with the packhorse, had pulled up in front of the cottage. Forcing a smile, Devereau indicated the earl. 'This is my friend of whom I spoke last year,' he said. 'Robert Preston, Earl of Yarville.'

The earl dismounted and bowed gravely to Mandy who curtsied. Morgan acknowledged the introduction with an equally grave inclination of his head. The captain's smile faded. The unfriendly atmosphere, so different from his expectations, confused and worried him. 'We are on our way to Dr Middleton,' he explained. 'We've been granted land higher up the valley beyond his property so we shall be neighbours, you see, Morgan.' He tried one more smile. 'We shall also be good friends, I hope.'

Morgan's answer was a polite rebuff. 'That would hardly be fitting, I think, sir,' he said, shaking his head regretfully. 'My wife and I are convicted felons, look you. We would never presume to have the friendship of gentlemen like yourselves. But my smithy is at your service and such skills as I possess you are welcome to call on just as Dr Middleton and Mr Weatherby do.'

Against such resolute unfriendliness the captain felt helpless. 'Well,' he said with a final effort at geniality, 'I suppose we had best be on our way.' He prepared to remount. 'We have some important papers from the Governor for Dr Middleton. One of them concerns your friend, Rob. I was hoping you could tell us where to find him.'

He swung himself into the saddle as he spoke and was surprised when Mandy ran towards him and grasped his horse's bridle. 'What makes ye think we ken aught of that wee devil?' she demanded. 'Morgan Jones and I opened our hearts to yon laddie and how did he repay us? He thought more of his black friends than he did of us!'

Devereau tried to hide his bewilderment at this outburst. He looked hopefully at Morgan but got no help there. 'The likes of us, sir,' the blacksmith said coldly, 'can't afford to concern ourselves with the likes of him, us being at the Governor's mercy and pleasure and me with a ticket-of-leave as could be taken from me. He would have more sense than to show himself hereabouts. He left these parts a twelvemonth or more since and we've not seen hide nor hair of him from that day to this.'

The captain's reception an hour later by Dr Middleton was a good deal warmer. Greetings and introductions over, the three men sat around the big table in the centre of the room which served the doctor for all purposes.

'Did you call on the Weatherbys on your way?' Middleton asked.

'We admired their new house from a distance,' Devereau replied with a quick smile. 'I felt

189

sure Mrs Weatherby would want notice of a visit from a peer of the realm.'

Middleton laughed. 'Then you have explained about our neighbours, the Weatherbys? According to Mrs Weatherby,' he went on for the earl's benefit, 'the social system is ordained by God and everyone has his or her fixed place, from His Majesty the King right down to his humblest subject.' He became suddenly serious. 'And in her estimation, I have no doubt, the lowest and humblest subject under the Crown would be the boy, Rob.'

Amusement faded from the earl's face. 'Yes,' he agreed in a faintly disapproving tone, 'I expect you are right.'

'Oh, Charles will tell you the same,' the doctor blundered on cheerfully. 'Even though Rob and his black friends saved her own children from Reilly's tender mercies, to Mrs Weatherby the boy is scarcely to be regarded as human.'

There was an awkward silence, broken by the captain asking bluntly, 'Do you happen to know where the boy can be found?'

Middleton looked at him with serious eyes. 'If I did,' he replied coolly, 'it would be my duty as a magistrate to arrest him — as you yourself reminded me once in the case of his friend, Murringoo. And much good came of that!'

'Many things have changed since then,' the captain replied, a little put out by the implied rebuke. 'A great deal can happen in a year.'

'Nothing has changed for Rob and Murringoo,' Middleton pointed out. 'There are two rewards to be claimed now and that ambitious sergeant you brought up here with you is determined to claim both of them. Three times in the past twelve months he's been up here with his troopers, harassing Morgan and Mandy — and me, too, for that matter. Now you come, asking the same question.'

The doctor's attitude had changed subtly since the enquiry about Rob and both men sensed in his manner the same strange evasiveness they had come up against at the blacksmith's cottage. 'You're out of uniform now, Charles,' Middleton went on, 'so you've no longer any professional interest in catching outlaws and so far as I, as a magistrate am concerned, I hope I never set eyes on those two again. You see, I can't forget the service they rendered to us in the valley by getting rid of Reilly and then leaving us in peace, for there hasn't been a sign of the natives since you went away.' Again an uncomfortable silence fell. 'I'm sorry if I seem to have been lecturing you but I feel strongly about the outlawing of Rob and his friend, Murringoo, as you've no doubt gathered.'

Devereau rose and picked up a saddle bag he had dropped by the door. 'We came up here with high hopes,' he said as he unbuckled one of the flaps. He drew out a roll of paper bound with pink tape to which a few fragments of red sealing wax still adhered and tossed it on to the table. 'These come from the Governor in Sydney — not that they are of any value now.'

Middleton unrolled the two documents, flattened them carefully and bent over them, frowning. As he read, his eyebrows rose and his forehead creased in delighted surprise. 'These,' he exclaimed, stabbing the documents with a

191

forefinger, 'are free pardons for Rob and Murringoo!'

'Yes,' Devereau responded casually, 'for what they're worth now since both have vanished into thin air.'

'Ah! But you don't understand!' the doctor cried jubilantly. 'These documents could make all the difference in the world! A free pardon for his friend, Murringoo, will do more than anything else to bring Rob back into the open...' He broke off, wondering if his listeners had realised what he had just let slip. Then he realised that it no longer mattered.

The earl looked at him with renewed interest. 'You do know something then? Something of the boy's whereabouts?'

Middleton beamed at his visitors. 'Of course I know where he is! Why the devil didn't you come straight out with it instead of letting me make a damned fool of myself? I had to lie because I had no idea why you wanted to find the boy and I had to protect him as well as Morgan and Mandy. Don't you see? Thats why *they* lied to you. You must have frightened them half to death with your enquiries, just as that damned sergeant did a couple of weeks ago.'

'But what have they to hide?' Devereau asked in a puzzled tone.

The doctor's eyes were sparkling with excitement. 'Rob, of course! He lives with them!' He laughed outright as astonishment and disbelief gave way to delight in the faces of his listeners. 'I'm not supposed to know he's there, of course. They wouldn't tell me because I'm the local magistrate and they think it would put me in a false position.'

'Then how did you find out?' the captain asked.

'My suspicions were aroused when Mandy asked me to buy a book for her on one of my visits to Newcastle. She said she needed an easy school book to teach her husband to read. But I happened to know that Morgan could read already and that he had, long before, promised to teach Rob to read. So I put two and two together.'

'But are you quite sure the boy is there?' the earl enquired anxiously.

'He's there sure enough!' Middleton regarded his questioner with amusement. 'Why should you of all people be so concerned about the lad?'

The earl looked him steadily in the eyes. 'He is my son,' he replied simply.

Middleton looked away, certain he had misheard and afraid to respond for fear of saying something out of place. He glanced across at Devereau for guidance, half expecting him to be smiling but his look was returned with a perfectly straight face.

'It is true, James,' Devereau said soberly. 'We have absolute proof that Rob is the Earl of Yarville's sole son and heir.'

Chapter 28

Father and Son

The earl was all for riding back to claim his son at once. 'No, no, no! That would never do!' Dr Middleton exclaimed. He was still confused and a little stunned by the story he had just heard. 'I'm sorry, but it's not going to be so easy and straight-forward as that! I understand your eagerness to meet the boy but it's going to take a great deal of diplomacy.'

'I don't understand. I am his father. Why should he not accept me?'

'Then you must try to understand that ever since the death of his mother and right up until a year or so ago, Rob had no reason to respect or trust or even like any member of the white race. Morgan and Mandy are in the delicate process of changing this attitude but don't ever forget that it was the blacks who first taught him the meaning of friendship and security when he was just a helpless little boy and it's to them he'll turn again if we threaten his security now with Morgan and his wife.'

'Then how am I to get to know him?'

'That is the question to which I am trying to find an answer,' Middleton went on seriously.

'To Rob you are a "swell", a "silvertail" of which the unfortunate Mrs Weatherby, whom Rob despises, is the personification. You see, you have a great social handicap to overcome.' The earl looked bewildered. While he set no great store himself on social position, he had never before had it presented to him upside down in this way. 'Now your position, of course, is not to be compared with that lady's but it's not going to be easy to make Rob understand the difference between you.' He stopped with a satisfied smile. 'But I think the difficulty may be overcome.'

'How?' Devereau asked.

Middleton picked up one of the documents. 'With this,' he replied confidently. 'Tonight, as soon as it is dark, we'll pay Mr and Mrs Morgan Jones a surprise visit. I shall go in alone and show them this — Murringoo's pardon signed and sealed by His Excellency the Governor himself. I shall explain who obtained it and brought it here and we shall have made a good start, I think.'

'But what of his own pardon?' the earl asked. 'Surely he'll be even more pleased about that?'

'Oh, I shall show him that, too, of course, but it's not so important. You see, Rob believes he has done nothing for which he could be pardoned. He stood by a friend in trouble, that was all. Only our white man's law would regard that as a crime.'

That evening the three men approached Morgan's cottage stealthily, walking their horses and tethering them in the trees. Lamplight glowed yellow between the boards of the shutter over the kitchen window, beneath which a wagon with one wheel removed was propped up on an improvised

195

jack. Middleton pointed to it. 'You two stand over there,' he ordered quietly as a soft murmur of conversation floated to them on the still night air. 'You'll be close enough to the window to hear what happens when I knock on the door.'

The voices from the cottage became silent as the doctor's knock sounded, followed by his reassuring voice. 'It's only me, Morgan! No need to hide Rob away. I know he's there, I heard him.' No sound came from within. 'Trust me, Morgan,' the doctor called. 'You know I only mean well for the boy.'

Suddenly the quiet of the night time bush was shattered by the crashing of the wooden window shutter as it slammed back against the wall of the cottage. Rob's crouched figure was outlined against the lamplight in the window as he leaped out. He landed, stumbled and staggered into the arms of the captain. Struggling violently, he would have broken free if the earl had not joined the fray. At last he stood, furious and frustrated, gripped between the two men.

'Stinking pigs!' he panted as Middleton ran towards them, closely followed by Morgan and Mandy. 'They gulled ye, Morgan! They ain't come to look at no land. They come to get me and Murringoo. Look!' He struggled again to show that he was being firmly held.

'Rob, listen to me...!' the doctor began.

'Stow yer gab!' the boy yelled at him. 'It was youse brung 'em here. Ye nosed me out first then sang to these here traps. But they ain't going to take me, see? I ain't glocky!'

'Rob, please listen...' Middleton tried again.

With a contemptuous toss of his head the boy shouted a few words in their Aboriginal language — they all turned and found themselves facing half a dozen armed black men.

'Rob!' Mandy cried anxiously. 'What are these people doing here?'

'They come for me,' Rob answered. 'I seen Murringoo down by the river today. I told him I was coming back to live with 'em till these here traps was gone away, like you and Morgan said. He told me as some of 'em would wait to show me where they was camped now.' He twisted his head from side to side, looking scornfully at the two men holding him. 'Take yer dooks off of me!' he ordered sharply.

'You must listen, Rob,' the doctor started desperately for the third time.

The boy ignored him. 'Take yer dooks off of me!' he repeated menacingly, 'unless ye wants to feel them spears in ye.' He made no effort to move when he was released but stood, impudently self-confident, straightening and smoothing his crumpled shirt.

'You're quite wrong, Rob,' Devereau said, 'we haven't come to arrest you. You're no longer wanted by the law. I brought your father here to meet you.'

The boy stopped brushing his sleeve and turned to face the speaker. 'I ain't got no bloody father!' he snapped.

'Oh, yes you have. He's standing right behind you.'

Rob turned to the earl. He looked him up and down insolently and laughed. 'I never seen him before.'

'And he's never seen you before either,' Middleton put in quickly, 'but you're his son, nevertheless.'

'Ye're a liar!' Rob accused him angrily. Suddenly Mandy stood before him. 'I'll no' have ye speak so to the doctor!' she exclaimed. 'I've no notion what he means but he's no' a liar and ye'll kindly beg his pardon.'

'Call off your friends, Rob, and come back inside so we can explain what has happened,' Middleton said.

'No!' the boy replied firmly. 'I'm off with them. I ain't staying here while them two swells is here.'

'Ah, that's a great pity,' Middleton replied. 'In that case you won't see the free pardons your father brought with him from the Governor in Sydney — one for Murringoo and another for you.'

'A free pardon for Rob, is it?' Morgan asked incredulously. 'No price on his head to bring the troopers after him now?'

The doctor pulled the documents from his pocket and held them up. 'See for yourself! Any trooper who lays a hand on Rob or Murringoo from this time on will have to answer to me for it!'

Morgan clapped an arm around Rob's shoulder. 'Did you hear that, boyo?' he cried happily. 'Free as a bird you are now!'

Rob seemed not to hear him. He was staring sceptically at Middleton. 'And Murringoo?' he asked doubtfully. 'Them traps can't hunt him down no more neither?'

'Murringoo is as free a man as I am and no one may touch him without breaking the law. If you'll come inside, Morgan shall read out both documents your father was given by the Governor himself.'

A few minutes later as Morgan finished reading all eyes turned to Rob.

'Why'd he do it?' Rob asked suspiciously.

'You are my son. What more reason should I need?'

The boy's eyes blazed with sudden anger. 'If he's my old man, why did he leave my mam, then? Why did he send her to that bloody Factory? To hell with him!' he shouted.

'It was not your father's doing, Rob,' Middleton said sternly. 'He was told a lie. He was told your mother had run away. He believed her dead. He never dreamed she had been transported for a crime she didn't commit.'

Rob glowered at his father across the table. 'Then how'd he nose me out?'

'It was Captain Devereau who found out the truth about you, quite by accident. And the truth is, my young friend, that you are the sole son and heir of the Right Honourable Robert Preston, Earl of Yarville and there is nothing in the world you can do to alter that fact.'

The faces of Mandy and Morgan were wonderful to behold as they stared at Rob. He stared back at them anxiously. 'That don't mean nothink!' he retorted scornfully. 'I ain't no bloody silvertail. I'm currency, I am!' He glared defiantly at his father. 'I ain't going nowhere with youse! Youse ain't my old man and if you was I'd hate your guts for what you done to my mam!'

Before anyone could stop him he had run to the door, flung it open and rushed out into the night.

'Should we not go after him?' the earl asked anxiously.

'He's gone to talk with his black friends,' Morgan said. 'He'll come to no harm with them. Before you came here tonight we told him he'd be safer with the Indians for a spell, us having no notion of your true intent. We thought it best, look you, for him to be hid safe away till you left the valley.'

A new vitality seemed to have taken possession of the earl. 'Tomorrow we shall continue up the valley to inspect our land,' he said in a businesslike voice. 'By the time we return, my son may be here waiting for us, if not we must find him — and find him we shall. Make no mistake about that!' His air of brisk authority changed as he turned to Mandy. 'I have to thank you and your husband, m'am, for the loving care you have given my son which leaves me for ever in your debt.'

He held out his hand to Morgan, smiling. The blacksmith grasped it eagerly and pumped it as vigorously as he had ever pumped the leather bellows of his forge.

Chapter 29

Decision

Five riders — three gentlemen followed by their two servants — cantered along the river bank with the last rays of the setting sun flashing into their eyes. Captain Devereau pulled down the peak of his military forage cap. 'Shall we reach your place before dark, James?' he called over his shoulder.

Dr Middleton, riding beside the earl, looked around him. 'This will be part of your land,' he replied. 'I'm not familiar with this reach of the river but we can't be more than five or six miles from home now.'

His companion appeared deep in thought. 'This is the seventh day we've been away,' he said as if to himself. He looked hopefully at Middleton. 'The boy should be back by now, don't you think?'

'Possibly,' the doctor replied after a brief hesitation. 'That is, if he's going to come back at all. That is something you may have to face, I'm afraid.'

'I shall find him,' the earl replied with quiet confidence.

'Rob is a free spirit,' Middleton went on. 'To him, the life of a gentleman seems more confined and restricted than that of a convict. He knows it's

201

simple enough to knock the rivets out of a set of leg irons but it's not so simple to rid yourself of the burden of being a gentleman.'

'Then what do you honestly think he will do?'

'It's going to be the most difficult decision of his life. You asked for my honest opinion, Robert, and I'm a realist. I believe he'll be guided by his black friends.'

Their steady canter broke down to a walk as they began to climb some low hills lining the bank of the river. The captain was in the lead and, as he reached the top, his horse reared and swung around in fright. He reined it in quickly but before he could warn the others they were bunched around him and the cause of his abrupt stop was apparent.

Some thirty yards ahead, across their path, stood a line of armed and painted Aborigines. They stood, a menacing human wall each with his narrow bark shield and bundle of long, thin spears.

The five riders regarded the scene with alarm. The captain turned to look back but there was no escape in that direction now for the track behind them was blocked by another barrier of armed men. His hand instinctively sought the pistol holster on his belt.

Middleton grasped his arm. 'No!' he warned, 'If there's danger here we shall only get out of it by talking, not shooting. Let me handle this...' He gave his horse a reassuring pat as he spoke. 'That tall fellow in the centre is Murringoo, their fight leader, Rob's special friend and protector. He must know a few words of English.' He turned to face the tall Aboriginal leader. 'Murringoo!' he called boldly. 'You know who I am. What is the meaning of this?

Where is the white boy? His father is here. Do you understand?'

There was no answer but a slim young warrior, his body naked and painted from head to foot with black and white patterns, left the tall man's side and approached them very slowly, stealthy as a stalking cat. Only his painted face, eyeballs gleaming white, showed above the shield held close to his body. A long, sharp spear was pointing menacingly at the earl.

'Do we sit here and let them kill us?' the captain muttered.

The other black warriors were closing in slowly now, spears poised. The youth in front was no more than ten paces away and if he chose to launch his spear the earl would have little chance of avoiding it.

'Good God!' Middleton exclaimed suddenly. 'It's Rob!'

The youngster froze, then with a gesture of savage impatience, hurled the spear into the ground at the feet of his father's horse.

'What the devil are you up to, Rob?' the doctor demanded, angry with sudden relief. 'You know as well as I do that this kind of behaviour can lead to trouble.'

The boy ignored him. He looked up at his father. 'Ye got guts,' he conceded grudgingly. 'I give ye that in.' He turned to Middleton. 'I been took into here by them, see? I can live with 'em always, if I wants.'

The doctor's face showed his concern. 'Rob,' he said earnestly, 'you're too young, far too young, to know what you're doing. Are you going to turn your back on a miracle? Your father is a good man and he needs his son. Remember, he got a free pardon for Murringoo from the Governor. Have you told him?'

'He knows,' Rob said.

'Good! And what about you? What's it to be? Are you going to live in the bush with these people or are you going to take your rightful place as your father's son?'

The boy frowned. 'The old men reckon as the white man's way is for the white man and the black man's way is for the blacks... '

'They're wise old men, Rob, and you would do well to heed their advice.'

'But it's for me to say,' the boy went on, his old air of defiance returning, 'and I ain't going nowhere and that's me last word. This here is my country. I'm currency, I am! This here's my place, helping old Morgan with his smithy work and seeing to Miss.'

'But that's not going to be enough, Rob,' Middleton pointed out desperately. 'When you inherit your father's titles and estates you'll need to know a lot more than any blacksmith.'

'I think I may have a solution,' Devereau broke in. 'The lad is quite right. He is not ready yet. This is his country. Let him remain here, living with Morgan and his wife and when I take over our land further up the valley, I'll make myself responsible for his education.' He appealed to the earl. 'Give him a year or two, Charles. You can see how impossible it is now. He isn't ready yet but in the fullness of time you shall have Margaret's son, I promise you.

Chapter 30

New Dreams

It had taken some time and a series of quite breathtaking mental and emotional gymnastics before Mrs Weatherby recovered from the shock of learning the truth about Rob's parentage but recover she eventually did, though not without some disappointed tears when she heard of the earl's intention to return at once to England to attend to his changed family affairs.

'You must not be too upset, m'dear,' her husband had consoled her. 'After all, we now have Captain Devereau as a neighbour and he is very well connected, as you know. And in a year or so we shall see His Lordship again when he returns to visit his son. And think how much better placed we shall be to entertain him then.'

'What a pity the boy refused to come and live with us,' Mrs Weatherby responded feelingly. 'I could have taught him so much more than that blacksmith and McInnes.'

How lucky Rob is, thought Thomas privately, to live with Mandy and Morgan and learn to become a blacksmith.

Prudence sighed. 'Just fancy! He's really *Lord* Robin!'

'Who do you mean?' asked a perplexed Thomas. 'The Earl of Yarville?'

'No, no, no, you silly boy!' his mother chided him. 'The son of an earl is called a lord. I wish you would pay more attention when I try to teach you these important things!'

Poor Thomas was now thoroughly confused. 'Maggie Jackson's kid is a real *lord*?' he asked incredulously. 'Shall I have to bow to him and Pru to curtsey?'

Mrs Weatherby looked startled. 'Well,' she began uncertainly, 'I do suppose that under certain circumstances... '

'I don't believe it,' Thomas interrupted her. 'Morgan told me Rob's mother was a servant girl just like McInnes.'

'A lady's maid can hardly be called a common servant, Thomas,' his mother informed him sternly. 'She was, after all, the personal companion to the late earl's wife who was a lady of quality herself.' Thomas was silent. The social somersaulting that had gone on in the Weatherby household since Rob's astonishing elevation to the aristocracy had been too much for his simple, honest mind. 'But why you didn't tell us you had befriended his young lordship in Sydney is quite beyond my understanding,' his mother concluded regretfully.

Thomas looked at his sister accusingly and she frowned a warning back at him. 'I didn't think you'd approve, Mama,' he said.

Mrs Weatherby gave a soft, ladylike laugh. 'Oh, my dear child, how little you understand me! I may have appeared at times somewhat... how shall I put it...? "Unsympathetic" is really too harsh a word. You see, everything I did was for the boy's own good. I was simply trying to show him how people in the best society behave.' She smiled a prim, self-satisfied smile. 'In spite of all appearances to the contrary, I always recognised something special about that young man, something different — an unmistakable air of quite charming independence and authority, which is now explained by his breeding.'

'It was very condescending of the boy's father to thank Thomas,' Mr Weatherby declared complacently. 'Of course, he realised that had it not been for Thomas's friendly action in Sydney, his son might never have thought of stowing himself away in one of the wagons and coming with us, in which case his birthright might never have been discovered. What a pity you had not told us about your meeting with his young lordship in Sydney, Thomas.'

'I should rather have told you,' Thomas said, irked by the constant chiding on the subject, 'but Prudence took such a strong dislike to him and threatened to...'

'Oh, stuff and nonsense, Thomas!' his sister protested indignantly. 'I had nothing against him. I did my best to make friends with him. Surely even you noticed that.'

'In three years time,' Mrs Weatherby speculated dreamily, 'Prudence will be going on eighteen and his young lordship seventeen from what I have been told of his present age. Ah, well! A difference of only one year is of little consequence, I daresay...'